Chinese

PHRASE BOOK

Compiled by
LEXUS
with
Yu Mei Zhang
and
Tom Mitford

HARRAP
London Paris

First published in Great Britain 1990
by HARRAP BOOKS LTD
Chelsea House, 26 Market Square,
Bromley, Kent BR1 1NA

ISBN 0 245-54937-4

Reprinted 1990

Printed and bound in Singapore by
Intellectual Publishing Co.

CONTENTS

PINYIN

Pinyin is a commonly used method for writing Chinese in the roman alphabet. But since it is not a pronunciation system in the sense in which phrase books traditionally understand pronunciation systems, we have not used Pinyin in this book.

If you do come across Chinese written in Pinyin the following 'code table' will help you decipher how the Pinyin is pronounced.

consonants

c	like 'ts' in 'hats'
q	like 'ch' in 'chin'
x	like the 's-y' sound in 'this year'
z	like 'ds' in 'fads'
zh	like 'j' in 'James'

vowels and vowel combinations

a	as in 'rather'
ai	as in 'Shanghai'
ei	as in 'Beijing' or 'weight'
i	pronounced as in 'Maria' except in the following combinations: *ci, chi, ri, si, shi, zi, zhi* In these combinations the 'i' is pronounced as in 'sir' (see also page 6)
ia	as in 'yarn'
ian	as in 'yen'
iang	pronounced 'yarng'
ie	as in 'yet'
iu	as in 'yodel'
o	as in 'for'
ou	as in 'dough'
u	as in 'Zulu' (but in some cases as below for ü)
ui	is pronounced 'way'
uo	is pronounced 'war'
ü	as in 'few' (it's the French sound as in 'du')

INTRODUCTION

The phrase sections in this book are concise and to the point. In each section you will find: a list of basic vocabulary; a selection of useful phrases; a list of common words and expressions that you will see on signs and notices. A full pronunciation guide is given for things you'll want to say or ask and typical replies to some of your questions are listed.

Of course, there are bound to be occasions when you want to know more. So this book allows for this by giving an English-Chinese dictionary with a total of some 1,600 references. This will enable you to build up your Chinese vocabulary and to make variations on the phrases in the phrase sections.

As well as this we have given a menu reader covering about 200 dishes and types of food – so that you will know what you are ordering! And, as a special feature, there is a section on colloquial Chinese.

The section on China and Things Chinese gives cultural information about China as well as some notes on the language.

This book uses Standard Chinese and simplified characters.

Speaking the language can make all the difference to your trip. So:

祝好运！

jù hǎo yèwn!

good luck!

and

一路顺风！

éelù shùnfērng!

have a good trip!

PRONUNCIATION

In the phrase sections of this book a pronunciation guide has been given by writing the Chinese words as though they were English. If you read out the pronunciation as English words (and pay attention to the tones) a Chinese should be able to understand you. Some notes on the pronunciation system:

ao as in 'Mao'
ay as in 'day'
e, eh as in 'bed'
ee as in 'feet'
er as in 'her'
ew as in 'dew' (if you know French, it's the 'u' sound)
I as the 'i' sound in 'high'
j as in 'jockey'
ir for example in 'shir': if you say 'shred' slowly (sh-red) then 'shr' is the 'shir' sound
u as in 'Zulu'
y is always as in 'you' and never as in 'why'

TONES

What is difficult, and essential, are the tones. Words are pitched – almost sung – and if a tone is wrong, the meaning could be lost. These tones are familiar in English, but whereas in English they express surprise or hesitation or sharpness etc (oh?, no!, so what!, hey ho!), in Chinese they determine meaning.

There are four tones in Mandarin Chinese: high level (1st) ¯, rising (2nd) ´, low (3rd) ˇand falling (4th) `:

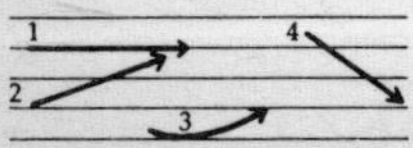

compare English:

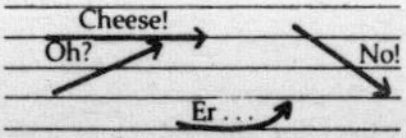

Some tones disappear in rapid speech.

GENERAL PHRASES

hello, hi
née hăo! 你好！

good morning
dzăosharng hăo! 早上好！

good evening
wănsharng hăo! 晚上好！

good night
wăn ān! 晚安！

pleased to meet you
jyèndào nĕe hĕn gāosyìng 见到你很高兴

goodbye
dzì jyèn! 再见！

cheerio
hwáytó jyèn 回头见

yes (*see grammar*)
shìrder 是的

no (*see grammar*)
bù 不

yes please
hăoder 好的

no thank you
bú yòngler, syèh·syeh 不用了，谢谢

please
chĭng 请

please do
bú kèrchee 不客气

GENERAL PHRASES

thank you/thanks
syèh·syeh
谢谢

thank you very much
fāycháring gănsyèh
非常感谢

you're welcome
bú kèrchee
不客气

sorry
dwàybuchěe
对不起

sorry? (*didn't understand*)
shémmer?
什么？

how are you?
née hăo ma?
你好吗？

very well, thank you
hén hăo, syèh·syeh
很好，谢谢

and yourself?
něe ner?
你呢？

excuse me (*to get attention*)
láo jyà!
劳驾！

how much is it?
dwōrshao chyén?
多少钱？

can I . . .?
wŏr kér·ee . . . ma?
我可以……吗？

can I have . . .?
wŏr kér·ee . . . ma?
我可以……吗？

I'd like to . . .
wór syărng . . .
我想……

where is . . .?
. . . dzì nălee?
……在哪里？

it's not . . .
bú shìr . . .
不是……

GENERAL PHRASES

is it . . .?
shìr . . . ma?
是……吗？

is there . . . here?
jèrr yŏ . . . ma?
这儿有……吗？

could you say that again?
nĕe nérng dzì shwōr ēebyèn ma?
你能再说一遍吗？

please don't speak so fast
chĭng bú yào jyărng jèrmer kwì
请不要讲这么快

I don't understand
wŏr bù míngbí
我不明白

OK
hăo ba
好吧

come on, let's go!
kwì dyĕn, wŏrmen dzŏ ba!
快点，我们走吧！

what's your name?
nĕe jyào shemmer míngdzìr?
你叫什么名字？

(*more polite*)
nĕe gwày·syìng?
你贵姓？

what's that in Chinese?
jèr dzì Jōngwénlee jyào shemmer?
这在中文里叫什么？

could you write that down please?
chíng syĕh éesyà
请写一下

that's fine!
hăo ba!
好吧！

I don't speak Chinese
wŏr búhwày jyărng Hànyĕw
我不会讲汉语

请勿乱踏草地	chĭngwù lwàntà tsăodèe	**keep off the grass**
请勿随地乱扔纸屑	chĭngwù swáydèe lwànrērng jĭr·syewēh	**no litter**
请勿随地吐痰	chĭngwù swáydèe tŭtán	**no spitting**
出口	chūkŏ	**way out**
公共厕所	gōnggòng tsèrswŏr	**public toilets**
公厕	gōngtsèr	**public toilets**
军事要地，请勿靠近	jēwnshìr yàodèe, chĭngwù kàojìn	**military zone, keep out**
禁止……	jìnjĭr . . .	**. . . forbidden**
禁止拍照	jìnjĭr pījào	**no photographs**
禁止停车	jìnjĭr tíngchēr	**no parking**
拉	lā	**pull**
男厕(所)	nán tsèr(swŏr)	**gents**
女厕(所)	nĕw tsèr(swŏr)	**ladies**
入口	rùkŏ	**way in**
推	twāy	**push**
危险	wāysyĕn	**danger**
外国人未经许可，禁止超越	wìgwórrén wày jīng syéwkĕr, jìnjĭr chāo·yewèh	**no foreigners beyond this point without permission**
油漆未干	yóchēe wàygān	**wet paint**

COMING AND GOING

airport
fāyjēechárng
飞机场

baggage
syínglee
行李

book (*in advance*)
yèwdìng
预订

coach
chárngtú chèechēr
长途汽车

bus
gōnggòng chèechēr
公共汽车

docks
mătó
码头

ferry
dùchwán
渡船

gate (*at airport*)
dērng·jēekŏ
登机口

harbour
gárngkŏ
港口

plane
fāyjēe
飞机

sleeper
wòrpù
卧铺

station
chērjàn
车站

taxi
chūdzū chèechēr
出租汽车

ticket
pyào
票

train
hwŏrchēr
火车

a ticket to . . .
dào . . . der pyào
到……的票

I'd like to reserve a seat
wór syărng yèwdìng éegèr dzwòrwày
我想预订一个座位

smoking/non-smoking please
syēeyēnchēw/fāy syēeyēnchēw
吸烟区 / 非吸烟区

a window seat please
chĭng dìng éegèr kàochwārng der dzwòrwày
请订一个靠窗的座位

which platform is it for . . .?
dào . . . dzì dèe jěe jàntí?
到……在第几站台？

what time is the next flight?
syà ēe hárngbān jéedyěnjōng?
下一航班几点钟？

is this the right train for . . .?
jèr shìr dào . . . der hwŏrchēr ma?
这是到……的火车吗？

is this bus going to . . .?
jèr lyàrng chēr dào . . . ma?
这辆车到……吗？

is this seat free?
jèr wàydzir yŏ rén dzwòr ma?
这位子有人坐吗？

do I have to change (trains)?
wŏr syēw·yào hwàn chēr ma?
我需要换车吗？

is this the right stop for . . .?
dào . . . dzì jèrlee syàchēr ma?
到……在这里下车吗？

is this ticket ok?
jèr jārng pyào yŏsyào ma?
这张票有效吗？

I want to change my ticket
wór syărng hwàn jārng pyào
我想换张票

thanks for a lovely stay
syèh·syèh nĕeder jāodì
谢谢你的招待

(*said to a group*)
syèh·syèh nĕemender jāodì
谢谢你们的招待

thanks very much for coming to meet me
fāycháռng gănsyèh nĕe lí jyēh wŏr
非常感谢你来接我

well, here we are in . . .
syèndzì wŏrmen dàoler . . .
现在我们到了……

有东西要申报吗？
yŏ dōngsyee yào shēnbào ma?
anything to declare?

请打开这个包，行吗？
chíng dăkī jèrger bāo, syíng ma?
would you mind opening this bag please?

办理登机手续，托运行李	bànlĕe dērngjēe shŏsyèw, twōryèwn syínglĕe	**check-in**
长途汽车站	chárngtú chèechēr jàn	**coach station**
起飞时间	chĕefāy shírjyēn	**departure time(s)**
请勿吸烟	chĭngwù syēeyēn	**no smoking**
出租汽车	chūdzūchèechēr	**taxi**
登机口	dērngjēekŏ	**gate**
电话亭	dyènhwàtíng	**public telephone**
非吸烟区	fāy syēeyēnchēw	**no smoking**
公用电话	gōngyòng dyènhwà	**public telephone**
国际航班	gwórjèe hárngbān	**international departures**
国内航班	gwórnày hárngbān	**domestic departures**
候车室	hòchērshìr	**waiting room**

候机室	hòjēeshìr	**departure lounge**
火车站	hwŏrchērjàn	**station**
站台票	jàntípyào	**platform tickets**
系好安全带	jèehăo ānchwéndì	**fasten seatbelts**
中国国际旅行社	Jōnggwór gwórjèe lĕwsyíngshèr	**China International Travel Service**
中国海关	Jōnggwór hĭgwān	**Chinese customs**
老人孕妇专座	lăorén yèwnfù jwāndzwòr	**reserved for the elderly and pregnant women**
列车到站时刻表	lyèchēr dàojàn shírkèrbyăo	**train arrival time(s)**
免税商店	myĕnshwày shārngdyèn	**duty-free shop**
男厕(所)	nán tsèr(swŏr)	**gents**
女厕(所)	nĕw tsèr(swŏr)	**ladies**
软席车	rwănsyéechēr	**soft seat carriage** (*more expensive*)
软卧车	rwănwòrchēr	**soft sleeper carriage** (*luxury*)
售票口	shòpyàokŏ	**ticket office**
吸烟区	syēeyēnchēw	**smoking**
行李寄存	syínglĕe jèetsún	**left luggage**
行李领取处	syínglĕe língchĕwchù	**baggage claim**
太平门	tìpíngmén	**emergency exit**
厕所	tsèrswŏr	**toilet**
问讯处	wènsyèwnchù	**enquiries**
硬席车	yìngsyéechēr	**hard seat carriage** (*cheapest seats*)
硬卧车	yìngwòrchēr	**hard sleeper carriage** (*cheaper sleeper*)

GETTING A ROOM

balcony yárng·tí	阳台
bed chwárng	床
breakfast dzăofàn	早饭
dinner wănfàn	晚饭
dining room tsāntīng	餐厅
double room shwārng·rén fárng·jyēn	双人房间
hostel lĕw·dyèn	旅店
hotel (*small*) léw·gwăn	旅馆
(*catering for Westerners*) fàndyèn	饭店
key yàoshir	钥匙
lunch wŭfàn	午饭
night yèh	夜
private bathroom sīrén syéedzăojyēn	私人洗澡间
reception jyēdìchù	接待处
room fárng·jyēn	房间
shower línyèw	淋浴
single room dānrén fárng·jyēn	单人房间
with bath dì yèwshìr	带浴室

do you have a room?
yŏ fárng·jyēn ma?
有房间吗？

just for one night
jĭr jù ēeyèh
只住一夜

do you have a room for one person?
yŏ dānrén fárng·jyēn ma?
有单人房间吗？

GETTING A ROOM

do you have a room for two people? yŏ shwārng·rén fárng·jyēn ma?	有双人房间吗？
I'm looking for a good cheap room wór syárng jăo éegèr tyáojyèn bútswòr yò pyénèe der fárng·jyēn	我想找一个条件不错又便宜的房间
I have a reservation wór ĕejīng yèwdìngler	我已经预订了
how much is it? dwōrshao chyén?	多少钱？
can I see the room please? wŏr nérng kànkàn fárng·jyēn ma?	我能看看房间吗？
does that include breakfast? jèrger jyàchyén bāokwòr dzăofàn ma?	这个价钱包括早饭吗？
a room overlooking the sea fŭkàn dàhĭ der fárng·jyēn	俯瞰大海的房间
we'd like to stay another night wŏrmen syărng dzì jù éeyèh	我们想再住一夜
we will be arriving late (*late at night*) wŏrmen jyārng shēnyèh dàodá	我们将深夜到达
(*later than planned*) wŏrmen jyārng wănsyeh shírhò dàodá	我们将晚些时候到达

can I have my bill please?
wŏr kér·ee fùjàrng ma?
我可以付账吗？

I'll pay cash
wŏr yòng syènkwăn fù
我用现款付

can I pay by credit card?
wŏr kér·ee yòng syìnyòng kă fùjàrng ma?
我可以用信用卡付账吗？

will you give me a call at 6.30 in the morning?
née dzăoshàrng lyòdyĕnbàn jyàosyíng wŏr, syíngma?
你早上六点半叫醒我，行吗？

at what time do you serve breakfast/dinner?
dzăofàn/wănfàn jée dyĕn?
早饭/晚饭几点？

can we have breakfast in our room?
wŏrmen kér·ee dzì dzìrjĕe fárng·jyēnlĕe yòng dzăofàn ma?
我们可以在自己房间里用早饭吗？

thanks for putting us up
syèh·syèh dwày wŏrmender jyēdì
谢谢对我们的接待

请勿打搅	chĭngwù dájyăo **please do not disturb**	电梯	dyèntēe **lift**
地下室	dèesyàshìr **basement**	一楼	ēeló **first floor**
		二楼	èrló **second floor**

GETTING A ROOM

饭店	fàndyèn	**hotel (*Western-style hotel*)**
服务台	fúwùtí	**reception**
工艺美术服务部	gōng·èe mǎyshù fúwùbù	**arts and crafts shop**
关	gwān	**closed**
招待所	jāodìswǒr	**hotel for Chinese officials only**
开	kī	**open**
旅馆	léwgwǎn	**hotel (*standard Chinese hotel*)**
男厕(所)	nán tsèr(swǒr)	**gents**
女厕(所)	něw tsèr(swǒr)	**ladies**
三楼	sānló	**third floor**
上	shàrng	**up**
下	syà	**down**
小卖部	syǎomìbù	**kiosk**
闲人免进	syénrén myěnjìn	**staff only**
餐厅	tsāntīng	**dining room, restaurant**
无人	wúrén	**free**
游艺室	yó·èeshìr	**recreation room**
有人	yǒrén	**engaged**

EATING OUT

bill
jàrngdān 账单

bowl
wǎn 碗

chopsticks
kwìdzir 筷子

dessert
tyénshír 甜食

drink
hēr 喝

eat
chīr 吃

food
shírwù 食物

menu
tsìpǔ 菜谱

restaurant
fàndyèn 饭店

salad
sèrlā 色拉

service
fúwù 服务

tea
chá 茶

waiter
jāodì 招待

waitress
jāodì 招待

water
shwǎy 水

a table for three, please
chíng jǎo ēejārng sānrén jwōr·dzir
请找一张三人桌子

we'd like to order
wǒrmen syárng dyěn tsì
我们想点菜

what do you recommend?
něe twāy·jyèn shemmer?
你推荐什么？

I'd like . . . please
wǒr yào . . .
我要……

can I have what he's having?
wǒr nérng yào éegèr hér tā éeyàrng der tsì ma?
我能要一个和他一样的菜吗？

EATING OUT

waiter/waitress!
jāodì!
招待！

could we have the bill, please?
wǒrmen kér·ee fùjàrng ma?
我们可以付账吗？

a pot of tea please
chǐng lí ēehú chá
请来一壶茶

tea with milk please
jyā nǐder chá
加奶的茶

that's for me
jèr shìr wór dyěn der
这是我点的

some more rice please
chǐng dzìlí ēesyēh měefàn
请再来一些米饭

a bottle of red wine/white wine please
chǐng lí ēepíng hóng pútáojyǒ/bí pútáojyǒ
请来一瓶红葡萄酒／白葡萄酒

chīngjēn fàndyèn **Muslim restaurant**	清真饭店
fàndyèn **restaurant**	饭店
fàngwǎn **restaurant**	饭馆
hǐwày tsāngwǎn **seafood restaurant**	海味餐馆
jyǒjyā **restaurant**	酒家
jyǒló **restaurant**	酒楼
myèngwǎn **noodle shop**	面馆
nán tsèr **gents**	男厕
něw tsèr **ladies**	女厕
sùtsìgwǎn **vegetarian restaurant**	素菜馆
tsèrswǒr **toilet**	厕所

CHINESE MENU READER

SOME BASIC MEATS

鸡	jēe **chicken**	猪肉	jūrò **pork**
牛肉	nyórò **beef**	肉	rò **meat (usually pork)**
鸭	yā **duck**	羊肉	yárngrò **lamb**
鱼	yéw **fish**		

RICE AND NOODLES

炒饭	chăofàn **fried rice**	炒米粉	chăoméefĕn **fried rice noodles**
蛋炒饭	dàn chăofàn **egg fried rice**	米饭	mĕefàn **rice**
面条	myèntyáo **noodles**	稀饭	syēefàn **rice porridge**

SOME BASIC MEALS AND FOOD ITEMS

包子 bāodzir
steamed dumplings with various fillings, normally including minced pork

春卷	chūnjwărr **spring rolls**	豆腐干	dòfu gārr **dried bean curd**

豆腐乳 dòfu rŭ
fermented bean curd

豆浆 dòjyārng
soya bean milk (typical breakfast drink)

豆沙包 dòshābāo
steamed dumpling with sweet bean paste filling

花卷	hwājwărr **steamed rolls**	馒头	mánto **steamed bread**

肉丸	ròwán	**meatballs**
咸菜	syéntsì	**pickles**
汤	tārng	**soup**
葱油饼	tsōngyóbǐng	**spring onion pancake**
油饼	yóbǐng	**deep-fried savoury pancake**
油条	yótyáo	**savoury doughnut sticks (typical breakfast)**

WAYS OF COOKING AND BASIC COMBINATIONS

炒……	chǎo . . .	**stir-fried . . .**
叉烧……	chāshāo . . .	**barbecued . . .**
茄汁……	chyéjīr . . .	**. . . with tomato sauce**
……丁	. . . dīng	**diced . . .**
冬菇……	dōnggū . . .	**. . . with mushrooms**
冬笋……	dōngsǔn . . .	**. . . with bamboo shoots**
芙蓉……	fúróng . . .	**. . . with egg white**
咖哩……	gāli . . .	**curried . . .**
干烧……	gānshāo . . .	**. . . braised with chilli and bean sauce**
宫保……	gōngbǎo . . .	**stir-fried . . . with peanuts and chilli**
蚝油……	háoyó . . .	**. . . with oyster sauce**
红烧……	hóngshāo . . .	**. . . braised in brown (sweet and soya) sauce**

MENU READER

滑溜……	hwályō . . . **stir-fried . . . with sauce**
火锅……	hwŏrgwōr . . . **. . . fondue**
火腿……	hwórtwăy . . . **. . . with ham**
炸……	já . . . **deep-fried . . .**
榨菜……	jàtsì . . . **. . . with pickled mustard greens**
鸡丁	jēedīng **diced chicken**
蒸……	jērng . . . **steamed . . .**
家常……	jyāchárng . . . **home-style . . .**
烤……	kăo . . . **roast . . .**
……块	. . . kwìr **. . . chunks, pieces**
辣子……	làdzir . . . **. . . with chilli**
麻酱……	májyàrng . . . **. . . quick-fried in sesame paste**
麻辣……	málà . . . **. . . with chilli and pepper**
木须……	mùsyēw . . . **. . . with eggs, tree-ear (an edible fungus) and day lily (lily flowers dried for cooking)**
……片	. . . pyèrr **sliced . . ., . . . slices**
肉丝	ròsīr **shredded pork**
三鲜……	sānsyēn . . . **'three-fresh' . . . (with 3 particular ingredients varying from dish to dish)**
烧……	shāo . . . **braised . . .**
什锦……	shírjĭn . . . **assorted . . .**

时菜……	shírtsì . . . **. . . with seasonal vegetables**
……丝	. . . sīr **shredded . . .**
笋炒……	súnchǎo . . . **stir-fried . . . with bamboo shoots**
虾仁……	syārén . . . **. . . with shrimps**
虾仁炒饭	syārén chǎofàn **fried rice with shrimps**
虾仁炒面	syārén chǎomyèn **fried noodles with shrimps**
香酥……	syārngsū . . . **crispy deep-fried . . .**
蟹肉……	syèrò . . . **. . . with crab**
糖醋……	tárngtsù . . . **sweet and sour . . .**
葱爆……	tsōngbào . . . **. . . quick-fried with spring onions**
……丸	. . . wán **. . . balls**
鸭块	yākwìr **duck pieces**
鱼片	yéwpyèrr **fish slices**
鱼香……	yéwsyārng . . . **stir-fried . . . in hot spicy sauce**
……元	. . .ywén **. . .balls**

COLD MEALS AS STARTERS

七彩冷拼盘	chēetsǐ lěrng pīnpárr **'seven colours' cold platter**
凤凰展翅	fèrnghwárng jǎnchìr **'phoenix with spreading wings' cold platter**
孔雀开屏	kǒngchwèh kīpíng **'peacock plumage' cold platter**

MENU READER

龙飞凤舞	lóngfāy fèrngwǔ **'dragon and phoenix dance' cold platter**
六宝大拼盘	lyòbǎo dà pīnpárr **'six treasures' cold platter**
三式拼盘	sānshìr pīnpárr **cold platter of three varieties of meat/vegetables**
什锦拼盘	shírjǐn pīnpárr **mixed cold platter**
五冷荤	wú lěrnghūn **cold platter of five varieties of meat/vegetables**

PORK

板栗烧肉	bǎnlèe shāorò **pork braised with chestnuts**
叉烧肉	chāshāo rò **barbecued pork**
青椒炒肉片	chīngjyāo chǎo ròpyèrr **stir-fried sliced pork with green peppers**
宫保肉丁	gōngbǎo ròdīng **stir-fried diced pork with peanuts and chilli**
红烧蹄筋	hóngshāo téejīrr **pig's trotters braised in brown sauce**
回锅肉	hwáygwōr rò **twice-cooked pork (first boiled then stir-fried)**
滑熘肉片	hwályō ròpyèrr **stir-fried sliced pork with thick sauce**
火锅猪排	hwǒrgwōr jūpí **pork chop fondue**
榨菜炒肉丝	jàtsì chǎo ròsīr **stir-fried shredded pork with pickled mustard greens**
酱爆三样	jyàrngbào sānyàrng **pork, pig's liver and kidneys quick-fried with bean sauce**
米粉蒸肉	méefěn jērngrò **steamed pork with rice noodles**

木须炒肉	mùsyēw chăorò	**stir-fried sliced pork with eggs, tree-ear (edible fungus) and day lily (lily flower)**
肉丝炒饭/炒面	ròsīr chăofàn/chăomyèn	**fried rice/noodles with shredded pork**
狮子头	shīrdzir tó	**'lion head' (large meatball stewed with cabbage)**
时菜炒肉片	shírtsì chăo ròpyèrr	**stir-fried sliced pork with seasonal vegetables**
笋炒肉片	súnchăo ròpyèrr	**stir-fried sliced pork with bamboo shoots**
糖醋排骨	tárngtsù pígŭ	**sweet and sour spareribs**
葱爆里脊	tsōngbào lĕejēe	**pork fillet quick-fried with spring onions**
鱼香肉丝	yéwsyārng ròsīr	**stir-fried shredded pork in hot spicy sauce**

CHICKEN AND DUCK

北京烤鸭	Băyjīng kăoyā	**Peking duck**
白斩鸡	bíjănjēe	**sliced cold chicken in a hot spicy sauce**
茄汁鸡脯	chyéjīr jēepŭ	**chicken breast with tomato sauce**
茄汁煎软鸭	chyéjīr jyēn rwănyā	**fried duck with tomato sauce**
冬菇/冬笋鸡片	dōnggū/dōngsŭn jēepyèrr	**chicken slices with mushrooms/bamboo shoots**
佛跳墙	fór tyào chyárng	**'Buddha leaps the wall' (chicken with duck, pig's trotters and seafood stewed in rice wine)**
咖喱鸡块	gāli jēekwìr	**curried chicken pieces**
宫保鸡丁	gōngbăo jēedīng	**stir-fried diced chicken with peanuts and chilli**

怪味鸡	gwìwàyrjēe **'strange-tasting chicken' (whole chicken with peanuts and pepper)**
红烧全鸭/全鸡	hóngshāo chwényā/chwénjēe **whole duck/chicken braised in brown sauce**
叫花鸡	jyàohwājēe **'beggar's chicken' (charcoal-baked marinated chicken)**
酱爆鸡丁	jyàrngbào jēedīng **diced chicken quick-fried with bean sauce**
酱爆鸭片菜心	jyàrngbào yāpyèrr tsìsyīn **sliced duck and green vegetables quick-fried with bean sauce**
樟茶鸭子	jārngchá yādzir **whole duck smoked with tea and camphor leaves**
辣子鸡丁	làdzir jēedīng **diced chicken with chilli**
珊瑚玉树鸡	shānhú yèwshù jēe **'coral and jade tree chicken' (with crab or ham on vegetables)**
时菜扒鸭	shírtsì páyā **braised duck with seasonal vegetables**
香酥鸭/鸡	syārngsū yā/jēe **crispy deep-fried whole duck/chicken**
葱爆烧鸭片	tsōngbào shāoyāpyèrr **sliced duck quick-fried with spring onions**

BEEF AND MUTTON

茄汁牛肉	chyéjīr nyóró **stir-fried sliced beef with tomato sauce**
灯影牛肉	dērngyǐng nyóró **'lamp shadow beef' (spicy hot beef, finely sliced, steamed then deep-fried)**
咖哩牛肉/羊肉	gāli nyóró/yárngró **curried beef/mutton**
宫保牛肉	gōngbǎo nyóró **stir-fried beef with peanuts and chilli**

蚝油牛肉	háoyó nyórò	**stir-fried beef with oyster sauce**
红烧牛肉/羊肉	hóngshāo nyórò/yárngrò	**beef/mutton braised in brown sauce**
酱爆牛肉/羊肉	jyàrngbào nyórò/yárngrò	**beef/mutton quick-fried with bean sauce**
家常焖牛舌	jyācharng mèn nyóshér	**home-style braised ox tongue**
烤羊肉串	kǎo yárngròchwàrr	**kebabs**
麻酱牛肉	májyàrng nyórò	**beef quick-fried in sesame paste**
麻辣牛肉/羊肉	málà nyórò/yárngrò	**stir-fried beef/mutton with chilli and pepper**
时菜牛肉片/羊肉片	shírtsì nyóròpyèrr/ yárngròpyèrr	**shredded beef/mutton with seasonal vegetables**
涮羊肉	shwàn yárngrò	**Mongolian fondue**
笋炒牛肉	súnchǎo nyórò	**stir-fried beef with bamboo shoots**
葱爆牛肉/羊肉	tsōngbào nyórò/yárngrò	**beef/mutton quick-fried with spring onions**
鱼香牛肉	yéwsyārng nyórò	**stir-fried beef in hot spicy sauce**

FISH AND SEAFOOD

芙蓉虾仁	fúróng syārén	**stir-fried shrimps with egg white**
咖喱鱿鱼	gāli yóyéw	**curried squid**
干烧桂鱼	gānshāo gwàyyéw	**Chinese perch braised with chilli and bean sauce**
干烧黄鳝	gānshāo hwárngshàn	**eel braised with chilli and bean sauce**
红烧鲤鱼	hóngshāo lěeyéw	**carp braised in brown sauce**

MENU READER

滑溜鱼片	hwályō yéwpyèrr **stir-fried fish slices with thick sauce**
家常鱼块	jyācháng yéwkwìr **home-style fish**
二吃大虾	lyǎrngchīr dàsyā **prawn heads deep-fried and bodies stir-fried**
时菜虾球	shírtsì syāchyó **prawn balls with seasonal vegetables**
虾仁干贝	syārén gānbày **scallops with shrimps**
蟹肉鱼翅	syèrò yéwchìr **shark's fin with crab**
糖醋鱼块	tárngtsù yéwkwìr **sweet and sour fish**
鱼香龙虾	yéwsyārng lóngsyā **stir-fried lobster in hot spicy sauce**

SPECIALITIES

八宝饭	bābǎo fàn **'eight-treasure' rice pudding (with eight varieties of fruit and nuts)**
叉烧包	chāshāobāo **steamed dumplings with barbecued pork fillings**
锅贴	gwōrtyēh **fried Chinese ravioli**
馄饨	húndūn **smaller Chinese ravioli in soup**
蒸饺	jērng-jyǎo **steamed Chinese ravioli**
家常豆腐	jyācháng dòfu **home-style bean curd**
麻辣豆腐	málà dòfu **bean curd with chilli and pepper**
麻婆豆腐	mápór dòfu **bean curd with minced beef in hot spicy sauce**

三鲜豆腐	sānsyēn dòfu	**'three-fresh' bean curd made with three ingredients which vary**
三鲜水饺	sānsyēn shwáy-jyǎo	**'three-fresh' Chinese ravioli ('three fresh' here usually means pork, shrimps and Chinese chives)**
砂锅豆腐	shāgwōr dòfu	**bean curd in stew**
烧卖	shāomì	**steamed dumplings open at the top, with sticky rice fillings**
水饺	shwáy-jyǎo	**Chinese ravioli**
松花蛋	sōnghwādàn	**preserved eggs**
小龙包	syǎolóngbāo	**steamed dumplings with various fillings, served on the bamboo steamers in which they have been cooked**
虾仁豆腐	syārén dòfu	**bean curd with shrimps**
鲜笋炒鸽片	syēnsǔn chǎo gērpyèrr	**stir-fried pigeon slices with bamboo shoots**

VEGETABLES

菠菜炒鸡蛋	bōrtsì chǎo jēedàn	**stir-fried spinach with eggs**
炒时菜	chǎo shírtsì	**stir-fried seasonal vegetables**
冬菇菜心	dōnggū tsìsyīn	**stir-fried oilseed rape with mushrooms**
冬笋扁豆	dōngsǔn byěndò	**stir-fried French beans with bamboo shoots**
海米白菜	híměe bítsì	**stir-fried Chinese cabbage with dried shrimps**
黄瓜炒鸡蛋	hwánggwā chǎo jēedàn	**stir-fried cucumber with eggs**

MENU READER

韭菜炒鸡蛋	jyǒtsì chǎo jēedàn **stir-fried Chinese chives with eggs**
烧二冬	shāo èr dōng **stir-fried mushrooms and bamboo shoots with vegetables**
素什锦	sù shírjǐn **stir-fried assorted vegetables**
西红柿炒鸡蛋	syēehóngshìr chǎo jēedàn **stir-fried tomato with eggs**
鲜蘑豌豆	syēnmór wāndò **stir-fried peas with mushrooms**
鱼香茄子	yéwsyārng chyédzir **stir-fried egg plant in hot spicy sauce**

SOUPS *(eaten at the end of the meal)*

八宝冬瓜汤	bābǎo dōnggwā tārng **'eight-treasure' winter marrow soup**
紫菜汤	dzǐrtsì tārng **seaweed and dried shrimp soup**
榨菜肉丝汤	jàtsì ròsīr tārng **soup with shredded pork and pickled mustard greens**
竹笋鲜蘑汤	júsǔn syēnmór tārng **mushroom and bamboo shoot soup**
木须汤	mùsyēw tārng **soup with sliced pork, eggs, tree-ear (an edible fungus) and day lily (lily flowers)**
三鲜汤	sānsyēn tārng **'three-fresh' soup (normally prawns, a meat and a vegetable)**
时菜肉片汤	shírtsì ròpyèrr tārng **pork and vegetable soup**
酸辣汤	swān là tārng **hot and sour soup**
西红柿鸡蛋汤	syēehóngshìr jēedàn tārng **egg and tomato soup**

DESSERTS

扒丝苹果	básīr pínggwŏr **apple fritters**
扒丝山药	básīr shānyào **yam fritters**
扒丝香蕉	básīr syārng-jyāo **banana fritters**
冰糖银耳	bīngtárng yín'ĕr **silver tree-ear in syrup (edible fungus)**
菠萝醪糟	bōrlwór láodzāo **pineapple in fermented glutinous rice**
莲子羹	lyéndzir gērng **lotus-seed in syrup**
三不粘	'sān bù jān' **'three non-stick' (dessert made from egg yolk, mung bean powder etc, – won't stick to your plate, chopsticks or teeth!)**
什锦水果羹	shírjĭn shwáygwŏr gērng **fruit salad**
杏仁豆腐	syìngrén dòfu **almond junket**
豌豆黄	wāndòhwárng **sweet pea cake**

HAVING A DRINK

bar jyŏbā	酒吧
beer péejyŏ	啤酒
coke (*R*) kérkŏkĕrlèr	可口可乐
dry gānder	干的
fresh orange syīnsyēn jéwjīr	新鲜桔汁
gin and tonic jīnjyŏ jyā kwáy·níngshwăy	金酒加奎宁水
ice bīng	冰
lemonade níngmérng chèeshwăy	柠檬汽水
red wine hóng pútáojyŏ	红葡萄酒
rice wine mée jyŏ	米酒
straight (*no ice*) bù jyā bīng	不加冰
sweet tyénder	甜的
vodka fútèrjyā	伏特加
whisky wāyshìrjèe	威士忌
white wine bí pútáojyŏ	白葡萄酒
wine pútáojyŏ	葡萄酒

let's go for a drink wŏrmen chèw hēr dyăr shemmer ba	我们去喝点什么吧
a beer please chĭng lí ēebāy péejyŏ	请来一杯啤酒
two beers please chĭng lí lyărng bāy péejyŏ	请来二杯啤酒
Chinese beer Jōnggwór péejyŏ	中国啤酒

imported beer
jìnkŏ péejyŏ
进口啤酒

a glass of red wine/white wine
ēebāy hóng pútáojyŏ/bí pútáojyŏ
一杯红葡萄酒／白葡萄酒

can I try a Chinese spirit?
wŏr kér·ee lí ēedyar Jōnggwór lyèjyŏ ma?
我可以来一点中国烈酒吗？

with lots of ice
dwōr jyā dyĕn bīng
多加点冰

no ice thanks
bú yào jyā bīng, syèh·syeh
不要加冰，谢谢

can I have another one?
wŏr kér·ee dzìlí ēebāy ma?
我可以再来一杯吗？

the same again please
chĭng lí éeyàrng der
请来一样的

what'll you have?
née syărng hēr shemmer?
你想喝什么？

I'll get this round
jèr tsìr wŏr fùchyén
这次我付钱

not for me thanks
wŏr búyào, syèh·syeh
我不要，谢谢

he's absolutely smashed
tā fā jyŏ fērngler
他发酒疯了

HAVING A DRINK

茶馆 chágwǎn **tea house** (*sometimes serving coffee*)

茶楼 cháló **teahouse** (*sometimes serving coffee*)

茶室 cháshìr **teahouse** (*sometimes serving coffee*)

酒吧 jyǒba **bar**

咖啡店 kāfāydyèn **café**

青岛啤酒 Qīngdǎo píjiǔ (*R*) (Chīngdǎo péejyǒ) **Qingdao beer**

崂山可乐 Láoshān kělè (*R*) (*Láoshān kěrlèr*) **Laoshan cola**

崂山矿泉水 Láoshān kuàng quán shuǐ (*R*) (*Láoshān kwàrng chwén shwǎy*) **Laoshan mineral water**

山楂酒 shānjājyǒ **liqueur made from berries**

杏仁霜 syìngrén·shwārng **non-alcoholic almond drink**

天府可乐 Tiānfú kělè (*R*) (*Tyēnfú kěrlèr*) **Tianfu cola**

五星啤酒 wǔxīng píjiǔ (*R*) (*wǔsyīng péejyǒ*) **five-star beer**

烟台味美思 Yāntái wèiměisī (*R*) (*Yēntí wàymǎysīr*) **Yantai vermouth**

音乐茶座 yīnyewèh chádzwòr **tea and concert** (*live concerts of all types of music at a café or teahouse*)

COLLOQUIAL EXPRESSIONS

barmy
shămào
傻冒

bird
gū·nyárng
姑娘

bloke
syăodzir
小子

nutter
yŏbìng
有病

pissed
shénjīng syēesyēe der
神精兮兮的

thickie
bèndàn
笨蛋

twit
shăgwā
傻瓜

great!
jēn bàrng!
真棒！

that's awful!
jēn dzāogāo!
真糟糕！

shut up!
hú shwōr
胡说！

ouch!
ī yō!
哎哟！

yum-yum!
hăo syārng a!
好香啊！

I'm absolutely knackered
wŏr lày·sirler
我累死了

I'm fed up
wŏr bú nǐfanler
我不耐烦了

I'm fed up with . . .
wŏr dwày . . . tăoyèn tòler
我对……讨厌透了

don't make me laugh!
byéh dò wŏr syào!
别逗我笑！

COLLOQUIAL EXPRESSIONS

you've got to be joking! nĕe bérng kī wánsyào!	你甭开玩笑！
it's rubbish (*goods etc*) pòr wányìr	破玩意儿
it's a rip-off chyāojúgàrng	敲竹杠
get lost! gŭndàn!	滚蛋！
it's a damn nuisance jēn tāmā der tăoyèn	真他妈的讨厌！
it's absolutely fantastic jwéler	绝了！

别吹牛！	byéh chwāynyó! **don't boast!**
大兵	dàbīng **soldier(s)**
还可以	híkér·ĕe **just so-so**
真的！	jēnder! **I don't believe it!**
老婆	lăopór **old lady, wife**
老外	lăowì **foreigner(s)**
聊天	lyáotyērr **to have a chat**
神经病！	shénjīngbìng! **crazy!**
他妈的！	tāmāder! **damn!, hell!**

GETTING AROUND

bike
dzìr-syíngchēr
自行车

bus
gōnggòng chèechēr
公共汽车

car
syǎo chèechēr
小汽车

change (*trains*)
hwànchēr
换车

chauffered car
lěw-yó chēr
旅游车

garage (*fuel, repairs*) chèechēr syōlěe chù
汽车修理处

map
dèetú
地图

motorbike
mórtwōr-chēr
摩托车

pedicab
sānlúnchēr
三轮车

petrol
chèeyó
汽油

return (*air only*)
líhwáy-pyào
来回票

single (*air only*)
dānchérng-pyào
单程票

station
hwǒrchērjàn
火车站

taxi
chūdzū chèechēr
出租汽车

ticket
chērpyào
车票

train
hwǒr-chēr
火车

tricycle
sānlúnchēr
三轮车

underground
dèetyěh
地铁

I'd like to rent a bike
wór syǎrng dzū ēelyàrng dzìrsyíngchēr
我想租一辆自行车

how much is it per day?
ēetyēn dwōrshao chyén?
一天多少钱？

when do I have to bring the bike back?
wǒr shemmer shírhò dáy bǎ dzìr·syíngchēr sònghwaylı?
我什么时候得把自行车送回来？

I'm heading for . . .
wǒr yào chèw . . .
我要去……

how do I get to . . .?
dào . . . dzémmer dzǒ?
到……怎么走？

REPLIES

一直朝前走
èejír cháochyén dzǒ
straight on

向左/右转
syàrng dzwór/yò jwǎn
turn left/right

就是那幢房子
jyò shìr nà jwàrng fárng·dzir
it's that building there

从那条路往回走
tsóng nà tyáo lù wǎrng·hwáydzǒ
it's back that way

左边的第一/第二/第三个
dzwǒrbyēn der dèe ēe/dèe èr/dèe sān·ger
first/second/third on the left

we're just travelling around
wǒrmen jǐr shìr dzì jèr ēe dì gwàrng·gwarng
我们只是在这一带逛逛

I'm a stranger here
jèrger dèefārng wǒr bùshú
这个地方我不熟

is that on the way?
nà jyò dzì yào jīnggwòr der lùshàrng ma?
那就在要经过的路上吗？

can I get off here?
wǒr kér·ee dzì jèrlee syàchēr ma?
我可以在这里下车吗？

thanks for the lift
syèh·syeh nĕe kīchēr
sòng wŏr

谢谢你开车送我

two tickets to . . . please
chíng mĭ lyărng jārng
chèw . . . der pyào

请买两张去……
的票

a ticket for tomorrow please
chíng mĭ ēejārng
míngtyēn der pyào

请买一张明天的票

what time is the last train back?
dzwày mòr ēebān
hwŏrchēr shemmer
shírhò hwáylí?

最末一班火车什么时
候回来？

can I use this ticket?
wŏr kér·ee yòng jèrjārng
pyào ma?

我可以用这张票吗？

can I have a refund for this ticket?
wŏr kér·ee twày jèrjārng
pyào ma?

我可以退这张票吗？

can I change this ticket?
wŏr kér·ee hwàn
ēejārng pyào ma?

我可以换一张票吗？

is this the right platform for . . .?
jèr shìr dào . . . der jàntí
ma?

这是到……的站
台吗？

is this train going to . . .?
jèr shìr chèw . . . der
hwŏrchēr ma?

这是去……的火
车吗？

GETTING AROUND

where are we?
jèr shìr nărr?
这是哪儿？

which stop is it for . . .?
dào . . . dzì nă ēejàn syàchēr?
到……在哪一站下车？

can I take my bike on the train?
wŏr kér:ee bă dzìr·syíngchēr dì shàrng hwŏrchēr ma?
我可以把自行车带上火车吗？

how far is it to the nearest petrol station?
dào dzwày·jìn der jyā·yójàn yŏ dwōr·yewĕn?
到最近的加油站有多远？

I need a new tyre
wŏr syēw·yào ēejir syīnlúntī
我需要一只新轮胎

it's overheating
mădá tì rèrler
马达太热了

there's something wrong with the brakes
shāchēr yŏ máobìng
刹车有毛病

汽车加油站	chèechēr jyāyójàn **petrol station**	起飞时间	chĕefāy shírjyēn **flight departure time(s)**
汽车修理厂	chèechēr syōléechărng **garage, repair shop**	请勿吸烟	chīng wù syēeyēn **no smoking please**

出租汽车	chūdzū chèechēr	**taxi**
出租自行车	chūdzū dzìrsyíngchēr	**bicycles for hire**
出站口	chūjànkŏ	**arrivals**
前面施工	chyénmyèn shīrgōng	**roadworks ahead**
单行线	dānsyíng syèn	**one-way traffic**
地铁	dèetyěh	**underground**
陡坡	dŏpōr	**steep hill**
一慢二看三通过	ēemàn èrkàn sāntōnggwòr	**first slow down, second look, third cross**
火车站	hwŏrchērjàn	**station**
站台票	jàntípyào	**platform tickets**
禁区	jìnchēw	**restricted area**
进站口	jìnjànkŏ	**departures**
禁止驶入	jìnjĭr shĭrù	**no entry**
禁止停车	jìnjĭr tíngchēr	**no parking**
禁止通行	jìnjĭr tōngsyíng	**road closed**
检票口	jyĕnpyàokŏ	**ticket barrier**
老人孕妇专座	lăorén yèwnfù jwāndzwòr	**reserved for the elderly and pregnant women**
列车到站时刻表	lyèchēr dàojàn shírkèrbyăo	**train arrival time(s)**
人行横道	rénsyíng hérngdào	**pedestrian crossing**
售票处	shòpyàochù	**ticket office**
小心路滑	syăosyīn lùhwá	**take care, slippery road surface**
通宵车	tōngsyāochēr	**all-night bus**
此路不通	tsīrlùbùtōng	**dead end**
铁路道口	tyĕlùdàokŏ	**level crossing**
问讯处	wènsyèwnchù	**enquiries**
5号码头	wŭhào mătó	**dock number 5**

SHOPPING

carrier bag
sùlyàodì
塑料袋

cashdesk
shōkwǎntí
收款台

cheap
pyénee
便宜

cheque
jīrpyào
支票

department
gwàytí
柜台

expensive
gwày
贵

market
shārngchǎrng
商场

pay
fùkwǎn
付款

receipt
shōjèw
收据

shop
sharng·dyen
商店

shop assistant
shò·hwòr·yewén
售货员

supermarket
chāojée shìrchǎrng
超级市场

I'd like . . .
wǒr yào . . .
我要……

have you got . . .?
yǒ . . . ma?
有……吗？

how much is this?
jèr dwōrshao chyén?
这多少钱？

the one in the window
dzì chú·chwārng·lee nà·éegèr
在橱窗里那一个

do you take credit cards ?
něemen jyēshò syìnyòng kǎ ma?
你们接受信用卡吗？

could I have a receipt please?
kér·ee gáy wǒr ēejārng shōjèw ma?
可以给我一张收据吗？

SHOPPING

I'd like to try it on
wór syărng shìrshir
我想试试

I'll come back
wŏr hwày dzìlí
我会再来

it's too big/small
tì dàler/syăoler
太大了/小了

it's not what I'm looking for
jèr bú shìr wór syărng·yào der
这不是我想要的

I'll take it
wór mĭsyàler
我买下了

can you gift-wrap it?
nĕe nérng tèe wŏr bāojwārng éesyà ma?
你能替我包装一下吗？

bĭhwòr dàló
department store
百货大楼

bĭhwòr gōngsīr
department store
百货公司

bĭhwòr shārngdyèn
department store
百货商店

chūkŏ
exit
出口

dà jyĕnjyà
sale
大减价

gùkèr jīrbù
no admission to customers
顾客止步

jyáokwănchù
cash point
缴款处

rùkŏ
entrance
入口

shírpĭn shārngdyèn
food store
食品商店

shōkwăntí
cash point
收款台

syénrén myĕnjìn
staff only
闲人免进

wénwù shārngdyèn
antique shop
文物商店

yíngyèh shírjyēn
opening hours
营业时间

SIGHTSEEING AND ENTERTAINMENT

Great Wall

The 'Chángchéng' is over 5000 kilometres long, crossing China from east to west as a defence against the northern nomads. The great emperor Qín Shǐhuáng linked earlier sections and completed the wall in the 3rd century BC.

Forbidden City

The 'Zǐjìnchéng' or grand palace in Beijing where the ancient Chinese emperors lived. Today it houses the National Palace Museum.

Terra Cotta Army

The 'bīngmáyǒng' is a lifesize model army guarding the tomb of emperor Qín Shǐhuáng since the 3rd century BC (this emperor was responsible for unifying the Chinese written language, legal and measurement systems).

Chinese Opera

This is one of the most popular forms of entertainment, with countless regional varieties, one of the best known being Beijing Opera or 'jīngjù'. Go to a park on a Saturday morning and you'll see crowds of (older) people playing traditional Chinese musical instruments and singing Beijing Opera.

Taìjí

Also known as 'shadow boxing', this is like a type of slow-motion aerobics and is very popular with older people. You will often see people doing taìjí in public parks, especially before breakfast.

GETTING AROUND

Two important points: 1. train travel is very popular, but there are no return tickets; 2. your ticket will only be valid on the train leaving at the time printed on it. Refunds (for which there is a small fee) are possible if application is made in good time. Train services (especially long-distance ones) are not that frequent, so missing a train could mean a delay of a day or so.

FESTIVALS

Chinese New Year

This is the most important Chinese festival, also known as the Spring Festival or 'chūnjié'. It is based on the lunar calendar and the date varies each year between the end of January and the middle of February. Celebrations usually continue for three days during which time families get together for sumptuous dinners. The climax of the festival is on New Year's Eve when, as the New Year's bell rings, people let off fireworks.

Lantern Festival

'Yuánxiāo jié', with dazzling displays of coloured lanterns of all shapes and sizes, is held at the first full moon after Chinese New Year and marks the end of the New Year celebrations. Typical festival food is 'tāngyuán', a sweet dumpling made of sticky rice pastry.

Dragon Boat Festival

'Duānwǔ jié', held on the 5th day of the 5th lunar month, commemorates the ancient poet and official Qū Yuán who drowned himself in protest at official corruption. Dragon boat races are held in his honour. 'Zòngzǐ' or rice balls wrapped in leaves are thrown into the water to appease the dragons there.

EATING

Most Chinese restaurants will give you chopsticks. It is quite in order to lift the bowl up to your mouth and use the chopsticks to push the food into your mouth. When you put your chopsticks down, lay them across the bowl. Don't stick them upright in the bowl, this looks like a temple-offering!

Eating in China is a major cultural activity. Meals are relaxed, with few 'do's' and 'don'ts'. It is only essential to enjoy yourself.

At the beginning of the meal, the host may apologize for the 'meagre spread'. You should not agree, but can contradict him, perhaps by saying 'hén hăo!, hén hăo' (very good). He will then invite the guests to start.

It is a good thing to make appreciative comments like 'hăo chī!, hăo chī!' (hăo chīr, hăo chīr – delicious, delicious) but often best not to enquire what you are eating. It is polite to have plenty, and you can watch the host and the other guests so as not to finish too fast.

When there are toasts, you hold the glass out in front of you. Though 'gānbēi' (gānbāy) means 'dry glass', a sip is fine.

If someone pours you a drink (including tea) it is polite to hold the cup or glass in both hands.

Towards the end of the meal, guests who have finished may say 'màn chī' (màn chīr – slow eat). This means 'I've finished, but please don't hurry'. The host may press you to take some more. If you've had enough to eat, you could say something like 'zhēn băole xièxiè' (jēn băoler syèh-syeh – I'm really satisfied, thank you).

There is never coffee at the end of a Chinese meal (though jasmine tea is often drunk). When the eating is over in a restaurant the guests go home.

CHINA AND THINGS CHINESE

LANGUAGE

There are many Chinese dialects, especially in the south, and though very similar in structure, they are often unintelligible outside the district where they are spoken. The Mandarin dialect of north China was chosen this century as the standard language (pǔtōnghuà).

Written Chinese is the same throughout the whole country. In the People's Republic many characters have been modified and the script is written from left to right, as in European languages. In Hong Kong and Taiwan the traditional characters have been retained and are still often written in columns, from top to bottom, right to left.

Some characters are derived from pictures:

竹 **bamboo**

马 **horse**

人 **man, person**

Some are a combination of pictures:

明 **bright (a sun** 日 **and a moon** 月 **)**

好 **good (a woman** 女 **and a child** 子 **)**

But most characters are made up of a 'sense part' (the radical) and a 'sound part' (the phonetic). The character for 'copper':

铜 (pronounced 'tóng')

combines the metal radical 钅

with the phonetic 同 tóng.

CHINA AND THINGS CHINESE

The character for 'oil':

油 ('yóu' – pronounced yó)
combines the water radical 氵
with the phonetic 由 yó

Chinese is a tonal language (see Introduction). The same syllable will have completely different meanings differentiated only by tone. For example:

妈	**mā** mother	马	**mǎ** horse
麻	**má** hemp	骂	**mà** tell off

CHINESE MEASUREMENT SYSTEM

China has some special measurements for everyday usage:

1 丈 zhàng (jàrng) = 10 尺 chǐ (chǐr) = 3.33 metres

1 尺 chǐ (chǐr) = 10 寸 cùn (tsùn) = 0.33 metres

1 里 (lǐ) = 500 metres

1 斤 (jīn) = 10 两 liǎng (lyǎrng) = 0.5 kilos

MONEY

bank
yínhárng
银行

bill
jàrngdān
账单

bureau de change
wìhwày dwày·hwànchù
外汇兑换处

change (*small*)
língchyén
零钱

cheque
jīrpyào
支票

credit card
syìnyòng kă
信用卡

exchange rate
hwày·dwàylèw
汇兑率

expensive
gwày
贵

foreign exchange certificate
wìhwày·jwèn
外汇券

pounds (sterling)
yīngbàrng
英镑

price
jyàgér
价格

traveller's cheque
lěw·syíng jīrpyào
旅行支票

how much is it?
jèr dwōrshao chyén?
这多少钱？

I'd like to change this into . . .
wór syárng bă tā hwàncherng . . .
我想把它换成……

can you give me something smaller?
nĕe nérng găy ēesyēh língchyén ma?
你能给一些零钱吗？

can I use this credit card?
wŏr nérng yòng jèrjŏng syìnyòng kă ma?
我能用这种信用卡吗？

can we have the bill please?
wŏrmen kér·ee fùkwăn ma?
我们可以付款吗？

please keep the change
chĭng lyósyà língchyén
请留下零钱

does that include service?
jèrger jyàchyén bāokwòr fúwùfày ma?
这个价钱包括服务费吗？

I think the figures are wrong
wŏr jwéder shùdzìr tswòrler
我觉得数字错了

I'm completely skint
wŏr ēefēn chyén yĕh máy yŏ
我一分钱也没有

Chinese currency is known as 'Rénmínbì'. The unit is the 'yuán' (*yew·én*) which is equal to ten 'jiăo' (*jyăo*) or 100 'fēn' (*fēn*). In spoken Chinese, however, a 'yuán' is called a 'kuài' (*kwì*) and a 'jiăo' is called a 'máo'. As a foreigner you will also change money into foreign exchange certificates (*FECs*) for use in tourist shops and hotels.

yuán
yew·én
元

jiăo
jyăo
角

fēn
fēn
分

kuài
kwì
块

máo
máo
毛

Jōnggwór rénmín yínhárng
中国人民银行
People's Bank of China (*dealing only with domestic currency*)

Jōnggwór yínhárng
中国银行
Bank of China (*dealing with foreign currency*)

rénmínbèe
人民币
name for Chinese currency (*shortened to RMB*)

wìhwày dwàyhwàn
外汇兑换
foreign exchange

ENTERTAINMENT

band (*pop*)
yewèh·dwày
乐队

Beijing Opera
jīngjèw
京剧

cinema
dyènyĭng·yewèn
电影院

classical music
gúdyĕn
yīn·yewèh
古典音乐

concert
yīn·yewèh
hwày
音乐会

disco
déesīrkēr
迪斯科

film
dyènyĭng
电影

folk music
mínjyēn
yīn·yewèh
民间音乐

go out
chūchèw·wán
出去玩

music
yīn·yewèh
音乐

play (*theatre*)
syèejèw
戏剧

pop music
tōngsú
yīn·yewèh
通俗音乐

rock music
yáogŭn·yewèh
摇滚乐

seat
dzwòrwày
座位

show
yĕnchū
演出

singer
gērchàrng·jyā
歌唱家

(*pop*)
gērsyīng
歌星

theatre
jèw·yewèn
剧院

ticket
pyào
票

are you doing anything tonight?
nĕe jīnwán yŏ shìr ma?
你今晚有事吗？

do you want to come out with me tonight?
nĕe jīnwán syărng hér wŏr èechĕe chūchèw ma?
你今晚想和我一起出去吗？

ENTERTAINMENT

what's on?
yĕn shemmer?
演什么？

have you got a programme of what's on in town?
née yŏ chérnglee dzwày·jìn der jyémù yĕnchū rìr·chérng·byăo ma?
你有城里最近的节目演出日程表吗？

which is the best disco round here?
jèr fùjìn nă·ēe·jyā déesīrkēr wúchărng dzwày hăo?
这附近哪一家迪斯科舞场最好？

let's go to the cinema/theatre
wŏrmen chèw kàn dyànyĭng/syèejèw ba
我们去看电影/戏剧吧

I've seen it
wór ĕejīng kàn·gwòrler
我已经看过了

I'll meet you at 9 o'clock at the station
wŏr jyódyĕn dzì chērjàn dérng nĕe
我九点在车站等你

can I have two tickets for tonight's performance?
wŏr nérng mí lyărng·jārng jīnwán yĕnchū der pyào ma?
我能买二张今晚演出的票吗？

I'd like to book three seats for tomorrow
wór syărng yèwdìng míngtyēn der sān·ger dzwòrwày
我想预订明天的三个座位

do you want to dance?
née syărng tyàowŭ ma?
你想跳舞吗？

do you want to dance again?
née syǎrng dzì tyào éetsìr ma?
你想再跳一次吗？

thanks but I'm with my boyfriend
syèh·syèhler, wǒr hér wǒr nánpérng·yǒ dzì·èechěe
谢谢了，我和我男朋友在一起

let's go out for some fresh air
wǒrmen chūchèw hwànhwàn syīnsyēn kōngchèe ba
我们出去换换新鲜空气吧

will you let me back in again later?
gwòr ēehway·r nēe hí hwày ràrng wǒr jìnlí ma?
过一会儿你还会让我进来吗？

电影院	dyènyǐng·yewèn **cinema**	台球	tíchyó **pool room**
剧场	jèwchǎrng **theatre**	影剧院	yǐngjèw·yewèn **theatre**
客满	kèrmǎn **house full**		

BUSINESS

business shēng·èe	生意
business card míngpyèn	名片
company gōngsır	公司
contract hértóng	合同
fax (*noun*) chwánjēn	传真
instalment fēnchēe fùkwǎn	分期付款
invoice fāpyào	发票
managing director jīnglěe	经理
meeting hwàyèe	会议
price jyàgér	价格
quote (*noun*) kīјyà	开价
target jǐrbyāo	指标
telex dyènchwán	电传
workflow schedule gōngdzwòr jìnchéng·byǎo	工作进程表

I have a meeting with Mr...
wǒr yào jyèn . . . syēnshēng
我要见……先生

may I introduce Mr . . .?
wǒr kér·ee jyèh·shào . . . syēnshēng ma?
我可以介绍……先生吗？

he is our technical director/sales director
tā shìr wǒrmender jèeshù jīnglěe/ twāysyāo jīnglěe
他是我们的技术经理／推销经理

can we send you faxes in English? wŏrmen nérng yòng Yīng·yĕw gáy nĕemen fā chwánjēn ma?	我们能用英语给你们发传真吗？
I'd like to have time to think it over ràrng wŏr kăolèw éesyà ba	让我考虑一下吧
we're very excited about it wŏrmen dwày jèr hén găn syìngchèw	我们对这很感兴趣
I'm afraid this is still a problem kŏngpà jèr réngrán shir éegèr wèntee	恐怕这仍然是一个问题
ok, that's a deal hăo ba, chéng jyāoler	好吧，成交了
excellent! tì hăoler	太好了！
let's drink to a successful partnership wày wŏrmender chénggōng hérdzwòr gānbāy	为我们的成功合作干杯！
it's a pleasure doing business with you hér nĕemen dzwòr shēng·èe fāycháng yéwkwì	和你们做生意非常愉快.

PROBLEMS

accident shìrgù	事故	
ambulance jyòhùchēr	救护车	
broken hwìler	坏了	
doctor ēeshērng	医生	
emergency jéeshìr	急事	
fire hwŏrdzī	火灾	
fire brigade syāofárng·dwày	消防队	
ill shērngbìngler	生病了	
injured shòsharng	受伤	
late chírdào	迟到	
out of order chū gùjàrng	出故障	
police jĭngchá	警察	

can you help me? I'm lost
něe nérng bārng ger márng ma? wŏr mée lù ler
你能帮个忙吗？
我迷路了

I've lost my passport
wŏr hùjào dyōler
我护照丢了

I've locked myself out of my room
wŏr chūmén wàrngler dì yàoshir
我出门忘了带钥匙

my luggage hasn't arrived
wŏr syíngleĕe hí máy dào
我行李还没到

I can't get it open
wór dă bù kī
我打不开

it's jammed
kă jùler
卡住了

PROBLEMS

I don't have enough money wǒrder chyén búgò	我的钱不够
I've broken down wǒrder chēr hwìler	我的车坏了
this is an emergency wór yǒ jéeshìr	我有急事
help! jyòmìng!	救命！
it doesn't work jèr dōngsyee hwìler	这东西坏了
the lights aren't working in my room wǒr fárng·jyēn der dērng hwìler	我房间的灯坏了
the lift is stuck dyèntēe gáy kǎjùler	电梯给卡住了
I can't understand a single word wǒr éegèr dzìr yěh tīngbùdōng	我一个字也听不懂
can you get an interpreter? něe nérng jǎo éegèr fānèe ma?	你能找一个翻译吗？
the toilet won't flush tsèrswǒr máyfǎ chōngshwǎy ler	厕所没法冲水了
there's no plug in the bath yèwchírlěe máy yǒ sīdzir	浴池里没有塞子
there's no hot water máy yǒ rèrshwǎy	没有热水
there's no toilet paper left máy yǒ shójǐr ler	没有手纸了

PROBLEMS

I'm afraid I've accidentally broken the . . .
hěn bàochyèn wǒr bù syǎosyīn nòng·hwìler . . .
很报歉我不小心弄坏了……

this man has been following me
jèr·rén èejír gēnjer wǒr
这人一直跟着我

I've been mugged
wǒr bày chyǎrng·jyéler
我被抢劫了

my handbag has been stolen
wǒrder shǒtéebāo bày tōler
我的手提包被偷了

公安局	gōng·ānjéw **Public Security Bureau (*Chinese police station*)**	
急诊室	jéejěnshìr **first-aid room**	
警察	jǐngchá **police**	
禁止……	jìnjǐr . . . **. . . forbidden**	
救护车	jyòhùchēr **ambulance**	
灭火器	myèh·hwǒrchèe **fire extinguisher**	
消防队	syāofárngdwày **fire brigade**	
小心！	syǎosyīn! **caution!**	
太平门	tìpíngmén **emergency exit**	
危险！	wāysyěn! **danger!**	

HEALTH

acupuncture jēnjyŏ	针灸	**disabled** tsánjeeder	残疾的
bandage bērngdì	绷带	**disease** bìng	病
blood syew·èh	血	**doctor** ēeshērng	医生
broken pèrngshārng	碰伤	**health** jyènkārng	健康
burn shāoshārng	烧伤	**hospital** ēe·yewèn	医院
chemist's yàofárng	药房	**ill** shērngbìngler	生病了
contraception bèeyèwn	避孕	**nurse** hùshir	护士
dentist yákēr ēeshērng	牙科医生	**wound** shārngkŏ	伤口

I don't feel well wŏr jwéder shēntĕe bù shūfu	我觉得身体不舒服
it's getting worse bìngchíng dzì jyājòng	病情在加重
I feel better wŏr jwéder hăosyeler	我觉得好些了
I feel sick wŏr jwéder hwày tù	我觉得会吐
I've got a pain here wŏr jèrr térng	我这儿疼
it hurts tòng	痛

HEALTH

he's got a temperature
tā fāshāoler
他发烧了

could you call a doctor?
nĕe nérng chĭng ēesherng ma?
你能请医生吗？

is it serious?
bìngchíng yénjòng ma?
病情严重吗？

will he need an operation?
tā syēw·yào dzwòr shoshù ma?
他需要做手术吗？

I'm diabetic
wór yŏ tárng·nyàobìng
我有糖尿病

have you got anything for ...?
née yŏ jìr ... der yào ma?
你有治……的药吗？

chĕwyào **dispensary** 取药

ēe·yewèn **hospital** 医院

ĕrbéehókēr **ENT department** 耳鼻喉科

fùchănkēr **gynaecology and obstetrics** 妇产科

gwàhào **registration** 挂号

jéejĕnshìr **emergency** 急诊室

Jōng ēekēr **Chinese medicine department** 中医科

kŏchyārngkēr **dental department** 口腔科

nàykēr **medical department** 内科

péefūkēr **dermatology** 皮肤科

syăoérkēr **paediatrics** 小儿科

wìbīn ménjĕnbù **foreign out-patients** 外宾门诊部

yĕnkēr **eye department** 眼科

SPORT

can we play table-tennis?
wǒrmen kér·ee dǎ
pīngpārngchyó ma?
我们可以打乒乓球吗？

I'm going jogging
wǒr yào chèw pǎobù
我要去跑步

I'd like to learn to ice-skate
wór syǎrng syew·éh hwábīng
我想学滑冰

how about a game of badminton?
chèw dǎ ēehway·r
yěwmáochyó
dzěmmeryàrng?
去打一会儿羽毛球怎么样？

can we use the tennis court?
wǒrmen kér·ee yòng
wǎrng·chyó·chǎrng ma?
我们可以用网球场吗？

we want to go on a bicycle trip
wǒrmen syárng gǎo ger
chéechēr lěw·yó
我们想搞个骑车旅游

I'd like to go and watch a basketball match
wór syǎrng chèw kàn
ēechǎrng lánchyósì
我想去看一场篮球赛

can I do shadow-boxing (taichi) with you?
wǒr kér·ee hér něe
èechěe dǎ tìjéechwén ma?
我可以和你一起打太极拳吗？

this is the first time I've ever tried it
jèr shìr wǒr dèe·ēetsìr
shìrjer wán jèrger
这是我第一次试着玩这个

THE POST OFFICE

letter syìn	信	**send** jèe	寄
parcel bāogwǒr	包裹	**stamp** yópyào	邮票
post office yójéw	邮局	**telegram** dyènbào	电报
registered gwàhàosyìn	挂号信		

how much is a letter to Ireland?
jèe dào ì·ěrlán der syìn dwōrshǎo chyén?

寄到爱尔兰的信多少钱？

I'd like four '1 yuan 6 jiao' stamps
wór syárng mǐ sìr jārng ēeyewén lyòjyǎo der yópyào

我想买四张一元六角的邮票

I'd like six stamps for postcards to England
wór syárng mǐ lyò jārng wǎrng Yīng·gwór jèe míng·syìnpyèn der yópyào

我想买六张往英国寄名信片的邮票

is there any mail for me?
yó wǒrder syìn ma?

有我的信吗？

I'm expecting a parcel from . . .
wǒr dzì děrng éegèr tsóng . . . lí der bāogwǒr

我在等一个人……来的包裹

THE POST OFFICE

can I send this express?
wŏr nérng jèe tèkwì ma?
我能寄特快吗？

can I send this airmail?
wŏr nérng jèe hárngkōng ma?
我能寄航空吗？

包裹，印刷品 bāogwŏr, yìnshwāpĭn **parcels, printed matter**

长途电话 chárngtú dyènhwà **long-distance telephones**

电报 dyènbào **telegrams**

开箱时间 kīsyārng shírjyēn **collection times**

营业时间 yíngyèh shírjyēn **opening hours**

邮票，挂号 yópyào, gwàhào **stamps, registered mail**

TELEPHONING

directory enquiries
cháhàotí
查号台

engaged
jànsyèn
占线

extension
fēnjēe
分机

number
dyènhwà hàoma
电话号码

operator
dzǒngjēe
总机

phone (*verb*)
dǎ dyènhwà
打电话

phone box
dyènhwàtíng
电话亭

telephone
dyènhwà
电话

is there a phone round here?
jèr fùjìn yǒ dyènhwà ma?
这附近有电话吗？

can I use your phone?
wǒr kér·ee yòng něeder dyènhwà ma?
我可以用你的电话吗？

I'd like to make a phone call to Britain
wór syárng wǎrng Yīng·gwór dǎ ger dyènhwà
我想往英国打个电话

I want to reverse the charges
wór syǎrng ràrng dwàyfārng fùkwǎn
我想让对方付款

hello
wày
喂

TELEPHONING

could I speak to Li?
chíng jāo·éesyà Lěe syēnshērng
请找一下李先生

hello, this is Simon speaking
wày, wǒr shìr 'Simon'
喂，我是 Simon

can I leave a message?
wǒr kér·ee lyó ger kǒsyìn ma?
我可以留个口信吗？

do you speak English?
née jyǎrng Yīngyěw ma?
你讲英语吗？

could you say that again very very slowly?
něe kér·ee fāychárng fāychárng mànder dzì shwōr ēebyèn ma?
你可以非常非常慢地再说一遍吗？

could you tell him Jim called?
něe nérng gàosu tā 'Jim' dǎgwòr dyènhwà ma?
你能告诉他 Jim 打过电话吗？

could you ask her to ring me back?
něe nérng chǐng tā gáy wǒr hwáy ger dyènhwà ma?
你能请他给我回个电话吗？

I'll call back later
wǒr gwòr ēehway·r dzì dǎ gwòrll
我过一会儿再打过来

my number is . . .
wǒrder dyènhwà hàoma shìr . . .
我的电话号码是……

76 32 11
chēe lyò sān èr yāo yāo
七六三二一一

TELEPHONING

just a minute please chíng děrng ēehway·r	请等一会儿
he's not in tā bú dzì	他不在
sorry, I've got the wrong number dwàybuchěe, wór gǎotswòrler hàoma	对不起，我搞错了号码
it's a terrible line jèr dyènhwà hěn bù chīngchu	这电话很不清楚

REPLIES

喂	**wày** hello
请等会儿	**chíng dérng hwǎy·r** hang on
你是谁呀？	**něe shìr sháy ya?** who's calling?

查号台	cháhàotí **directory enquiries**	公用电话	gōngyòng dyènhwà **public telephone**
长途电话	chárngtú dyènhwà **long-distance telephone**	火警、盗警、匪警	hwórjǐng, dàojǐng, fáyjǐng **09 – emergency number for fire, burglary and robbery**
电话簿	dyènhwàbù **telephone directory**		
一次四分	éetsìr sìrfēn **four fen per call**		

NUMBERS, THE DATE, THE TIME

0	líng	零
1	ēe	一
2	èr (but lyărng for time)	二
3	sān	三
4	sìr	四
5	wŭ	五
6	lyò	六
7	chēe	七
8	bā	八
9	jyŏ	九
10	shír	十
11	shír·ēe	十一
12	shír·èr	十二
13	shírsān	十三
14	shírsìr	十四
15	shírwŭ	十五
16	shírlyò	十六
17	shírchēe	十七
18	shírbā	十八
19	shírjyŏ	十九
20	èrshír	二十
21	èrshír·ēe	二十一
22	èrshír·èr	二十二
30	sānshír	三十
35	sānshírwŭ	三十五
40	sìrshír	四十
50	wŭshír	五十
60	lyòshír	六十
70	chēeshír	七十
80	bāshír	八十
90	jyŏshír	九十
91	jyŏshír·ēe	九十一

100	bǐ	百
101	ēebǐlíng·ēe	一百零一
200	lyárngbǐ	二百
202	èrbǐlíng·èr	二百零二
1,000	chyēn	千
2,000	lyǎrng·chyēn	二千
10,000	wàn	万
1,000,000	bǐwàn	百万
100,000,000	èe	亿

see also grammar section

1st	dèe ēe	第一
2nd	dèe èr	第二
3rd	dèe sān	第三
4th	dèe sìr	第四
5th	dèe wǔ	第五
6th	dèe lyò	第六
7th	dèe chēe	第七
8th	dèe bā	第八
9th	dèe jyǒ	第九
10th	dèe shír	第十

what's the date?
jīntyēn jěehào?
今天几号？

it's the first of June
jīntyēn lyò yewèh ēehào
今天六月一号

1994
ēejyójyǒsìr nyén
一九九四年

what time is it?
jéedyěnler?
几点了？

it's midday/midnight
syèndzì jōngwǔ/bànyèh
现在中午/半夜

it's one/three o'clock
syèndzì
ēedyěnler/sāndyěnler
现在一点了/三点了

it's twenty past three
syèndzì sāndyěn èrshír
现在三点二十

it's twenty to three
syèndzì chā èrshír
sāndyěn
现在差二十三点

it's half past eight/half past nine
syèndzì
bādyěnbàn/jyódyěnbàn
现在八点半/九点半

it's a quarter past five
syèndzì wúdyěn ēekèr
现在五点一刻

it's quarter to five
syèndzì chā ēekèr
wúdyěn
现在差一刻五点

at two/five o'clock
dzì lyárngdyěn/wúdyěn
在二点/五点

ENGLISH-CHINESE

A

a
(*see grammar*)

about (*approx*) 大概
dàgì

above 在……上面
dzì . . .
shàrngmyèn

accident 事故
shìrgù

acrobatics 杂技
dzájèe

acupuncture 针灸
jēnjyŏ

adaptor (*for voltage*) 变压器
byènyāchèe
(*plug*) 多用插头
dwōryòng
chātó

address 地址
dèejĭr

adult 大人
dàrén

aeroplane 飞机
fāyjēe

after 以后
ĕehò

afternoon 下午
syàwŭ

afterwards 后来
hòlì

again 再
dzì

against: I'm against it 我反对
wór făndwày

age 年纪
nyénjèe

agent 代理人
dìlĕerén

ago 以前
ĕechyén
three days ago 三天以前
sān tyēn
ĕechyén

agree: I agree 我同意
wŏr tóng·èe

AIDS 艾滋病
ìdzīrbìng

air 空气
kōngchèe

air-conditioning 空调
kōngtyáo

airmail: by airmail 航空信
hárngkōngsyìn

airport 飞机场
fāyjēechărng

alarm clock 闹钟
nàojōng

alcohol 酒精
jyŏjīng

alive 活着
hwórjer

all 所有
swóryŏ

allergic to
dwày . . . yǒ gwòrmǐn fǎnyìng 对……有过敏反应
allowed
yéwnsyěwder 允许的
all right: that's all right
syíng 行
almost
chàbudwōr 差不多
alone
dāndú 单独
also
yěh 也
altogether
éegòng 一共
always
dzǒngshìr 总是
ambulance
jyòhùchēr 救护车
America
Mǎygwór 美国
amp: 13-amp
13 ānpáy 13安培
and
hér 和
angry
shērngchèe 生气
ankle
jyǎobórdzir 脚脖子
another (*different*)
lìng éegèr 另一个
(*extra*)
yò éegèr 又一个
another beer
yòlǐ éegèr péejyǒ 又来一个啤酒
answer
hwáydá 回答
antibiotic
kàrngjēwnsù 抗菌素
antihistamine
kàrngdzǔān 抗组胺
antiseptic
fárngfǔjèe 防腐剂
apartment
dān·yewén 单元
appendicitis
lánwǎy·yén 阑尾炎
apple
pínggwǒr 苹果
appointment
yewēh·hwày 约会
apricot
syìngdzir 杏子
April
sìr·yewèh 四月
arm
gērbor 胳膊
arrest
dìbǔ 逮捕
arrive
dào 到
art
èeshù 艺术
artist
èeshùjyā 艺术家
ashtray
yēnhwāygārng 烟灰缸
ask
wèn 问
asleep
shwàyjáoler 睡着了
aspirin
āsīrpěelín 阿司匹林
asthma
syàochwǎn 哮喘

at
dzì 在
at the station
dzì chērjàn 在车站
at Xiao Wang's
dzì Syǎo Wárng jyā 在小王家
attractive
míréndér 迷人的
August
bā·yewèh 八月
aunt (*maternal*)
éemā 姨妈
(*paternal*)
gūmā 姑妈
Australia
Àodàlèeyà 澳大利亚
automatic
dzìrdòng 自动
autumn
chyōtyēn 秋天
awake
syǐngjer 醒着
awful
dzāotòler 糟透了
axle
jó 轴

B

baby
yīng·ér 婴儿
back
hwáy 回
go back
hwáy chèw 回去
come back
hwáy lí 回来
back (*of body*)
bày 背
bad
hwì 坏
bag
sùlyàodì 塑料袋
(*suitcase*)
syārngdzir 箱子
baggage check (*US*)
syínglěe jèetsúnchù 行李寄存处
baker
myènbāofárng 面包房
bald
tūtó 秃头
ball
chyó 球
bamboo
júdzir 竹子
banana
syārngjyāo 香蕉
bandage
bērngdì 绷带
bank
yínhárng 银行
bar
jyǒbā 酒吧
barber
lěefàdyèn 理发店
bath
syéedzǎo 洗澡
bathroom
syéedzǎojyēn 洗澡间
battery
dyènchír 电池
be
shìr; (*see grammar*) 是

beach
hǐtān 海滩

beans
dòdzir 豆子

beard
húdzir 胡子

beautiful
mǎylèe 美丽

because
yīnway 因为

bed
chwárng 床

bedroom
wòrshìr 卧室

bee
mèefērng 蜜蜂

beef
nyórò 牛肉

beer
péejyǒ 啤酒

before
dzì . . .
ěechyén 在……以前

begin
kīshǐr 开始

behind
dzì . . . hòmyen 在……后面

bell
jōng 钟
(*for door*)
líng 铃

below
dzì . . . syàmyèn 在……下面

belt
yāodì 腰带

bend
jwǎnwān 转弯

best: the best
dzwàyhǎo 最好

better
hǎo ēedyǎrr 好一点

between
dzì . . . jīrjyēn 在……之间

bicycle
dzìr·syíngchēr 自行车

big
dà 大

bill
jàrngdān 账单

bird
nyǎo 鸟

biro (*R*)
yewén·jūběe 元珠笔

birthday
shērngrìr 生日

biscuit
bǐnggān 饼干

bit: a little bit
ēedyǎrr 一点

bite (*insect*)
yǎo 咬

black
hāy 黑

blanket
tǎndzir 毯子

blind
syā 瞎

blocked
dǔjùler 堵住了

blond
jīnhwárngsèr 金黄色

blood
syew·èh 血

blouse
něwchènshān 女衬衫

blue
lánsèr 蓝色

boat 船
chwán

body 身体
shēntěe

boiled egg 荷包蛋
hérbāodàn

boiled rice 米饭
měefàn

bomb 炸弹
jàdàn

bone 骨头
gúto
(*in fish*) 鱼刺
yéwtsìr

book 书
shū

bookshop 书店
shūdyèn

boot (*shoe*) 靴子
syew·ēh·dzir
(*car*) 行李箱
syíngleesyārng

border 边界
byēnjyèh

boring 没劲
máy jìn

boss 老板
láobǎn

both 二个
lyǎrngger
both of them 他们二个
tāmen
lyǎrngger

bottle 瓶子
píngdzir

bottle-opener 开瓶子的
kī píngdzǐr
der

bowl 碗
wǎn

box 盒子
hérdzir

boy 男孩
nánhí

boyfriend 男朋友
nán pérngyo

bra 胸罩
syōngjào

bracelet 手镯
shǒjwór

brake 刹车
shāchēr

brandy 白兰地
bílándèe

brave 勇敢
yónggǎn

bread 面包
myènbāo

break 搞坏
gǎohwì

breakfast 早饭
dzǎofàn

bridge (*over river etc*) 桥
chyáo

briefcase 公文包
gōngwénbāo

bring 带来
dìlı

Britain 英国
Yīnggwór

broken 坏了
hwìler

brooch 胸针
syōngjēn

brother 兄弟
syōngdèe

brown 棕色
dzōngsèr

brush
shwādzir 刷子

bucket
tōng 桶

Buddha
Fór 佛

Buddhism
Fórjyào 佛教

Buddhist (*adjective*)
Fórjyào 佛教

building
fárngdzir 房子

Burma
Myěndyèn 缅甸

burn (*noun*)
shāoshārng 烧伤

bus
gōnggòng chèechēr 公共汽车

business
shērng·èe 生意

business trip
chūchī 出差

bus station
gōnggòng chèechēr jàn 公共汽车站

bus stop
chērjàn 车站

but
dànshìr 但是

butcher
ròdyèn 肉店

butter
hwárngyó 黄油

button
nyŏkò 钮扣

buy
mǐ 买

by
dzwòr 坐

by car
dzwòr chēr 坐车

C

café
kāfāygwărr 咖啡馆

cake
dàngāo 蛋糕

calculator
jèeswànchèe 计算器

calendar
rìrlèe 日历

calligraphy
shūfǎ 书法

camera
jàosyàrngjēe 照像机

can (*noun*)
gwànto 罐头

can (*verb*): **I/she can**
wŏr/tā nérnggò 我／她能够

I can't swim
wŏr búhwày yóyŏng 我不会游泳

Canada
Jyānádà 加拿大

cancel
chĕwsyāo 取消

Cantonese
(*adjective*) Gwărngdōng 广东
(*language*) Gwărng-donghwà 广东话

cap (*hat*)
màodzir 帽子

car
syăo chèechēr 小汽车

card (*business*)
míngpyèn 名片

careful: be careful!
syăosyīn! 小心！

car park
tíngchērchărng 停车场

carpet
dèetăn 地毯

carrot
húlwórbor 胡萝卜

cassette
héshìr tsírdì 盒式磁带

cassette player
lùyīnjēe 录音机

cat
māo 猫

cauliflower
tsìhwā 菜花

cave
shāndòng 山洞

ceiling
tyēnhwābăn 天花板

cemetery
mùdèe 墓地

centigrade
shèrshìr 摄氏

centre
jōngsyīn 中心

certificate
jèrngshū 证书

chain (*around neck*)
syàrnglyèn 项链

chair
ĕedzir 椅子

change (*small*)
língchyén 零钱

change (*verb*)
hwàn 换

change trains
hwàn hwŏrchēr 换火车

character
fārngkwìdzìr 方块字

cheap
pyénee 便宜

check (*verb*)
jyĕnchá 检查

check (*US: money*)
jīrpyào 支票

check-in
dērngjèe 登记

cheers!
gānbāy 干杯

cheese
nĭlào 奶酪

chemist
yàofárng 药房

cheque
jīrpyào 支票

cherry
yīngtáo 樱桃

chest
syōngkŏ 胸口

chewing gum
kŏsyārngtárng 口香糖

chicken
jēe 鸡
(*meat*)
jēerò 鸡肉

child
hídzir 孩子

chin
syàba 下巴
China
Jōnggwór 中国
China tea
Jōnggwor chá 中国茶
Chinese
(*adjective*)
Jōnggwor 中国
(*person*)
Jōnggwor·ren 中国人
(*language*)
Hànyěw 汉语
the Chinese
Jōnggwor rénmín 中国人民
Chinese-style
Jōngshìr 中式
chips
já tǔdòtyáo 炸土豆条
(*US*)
já tǔdòpyàrr 炸土豆片
chocolate
chyǎokèrlèe 巧克力
chopsticks
kwìdzir 筷子
Christmas
shèrngdànjyéh 圣诞节
church
jyàotárng 教堂
cigar
syewěh·jyā 雪茄
cigarette
syārng yēn 香烟
cinema
dyènyǐng yewèn 电影院
city
chérngshìr 城市
city centre
shìr jōngsyīn 市中心
clean (*adjective*)
gānjìng 干净
clean (*verb*)
dásǎo 打扫
clever
tsōngming 聪明
clock
jōng 钟
close (*verb*)
gwān 关
closed
gwānménler 关门了
closet (*US*)
gwàydzir 柜子
clothes
ēefu 衣服
clothes peg
ēefu jyādzir 衣服夹子
cloudy
yīntyēn 阴天
clutch
léehérchèe 离合器
coat
wì·ēe 外衣
coathanger
ēejyà 衣架
cockroach
jārnglárng 蟑螂
coffee
kāfāy 咖啡
cold
lěrng 冷
I've got a cold
wór gǎnmàoler 我感冒了
collect call
dwàyfārng fùkwǎn 对方付款

colour 颜色
yénsèr

colour film 彩色胶卷
tsǐsèr
jyāojwǎrr

comb 梳子
shūdzir

come 来
lí

come back 回来
hwáylí

come in! 请进
chǐng jìn

comfortable 舒服
shūfu

Communist Party 共产党
gòngchán·
dǎrng

Communist Party member 共产党员
gòngchándǎrng·
yewén

complicated 复杂
fùdzá

computer 计算机
jèeswànjēe

concert 音乐会
yīnyewèh·hwày

condom 避孕套
bèeyèwntào

congratulations! 恭喜！恭喜！
gōngsyěe!
gōngsyěe!

constipated 便秘
byènbèe

consulate 领事馆
lǐngshìrgwǎn

contact lenses 隐形眼镜
yǐnsyíng
yěnjìng

cool 凉快
lyárngkwɪ

corkscrew 开酒瓶塞的
kɪ̄
jyǒpíngsɪ̄der

corner 角落
jyǎolwòr

correct 对
dwày

cotton 棉花
myénhwā

cotton wool 药棉
yàomyén

cough 咳嗽
kérso

country 国家
gwórjyā

course: of course 当然
dārngrán

crab 螃蟹
párngsyèh

cream (*to eat*) 奶油
nɪ̌yó

credit card 信用卡
syìnyòng kǎ

crisps 炸土豆片
já tǔdòpyàrr

crowded 拥挤
yōng jěe

cry 哭
kū

Cultural Revolution 文化大革命
wénhwà
dàgérmìng

cup 杯子
bāydzir

cupboard 柜子
gwàydzir

curtain 帘子
lyéndzir

customs 海关
hīgwān

cyclist 骑自行车的
chée dzìrsyíngchēr der

D

dangerous 危险
wāysyěn

dark 黑暗
hāy àn

date (*time*) 日期
rìrchēe

daughter 女儿
něwér

day 天
tyēn

the day before yesterday 前天
chyéntyēn

the day after tomorrow 后天
hòtyēn

dead 死了
sǐrler

deaf 耳聋
ěr lóng

death 死亡
sǐrwárng

decaffeinated 去掉咖啡因的
chèwdyào kāfāyyīn der

December 十二月
shírèr·yewèh

deep 深
shēn

delicious 好吃
hăochīr

dentist 牙科医生
yákēr ēeshērng

deodorant 除臭剂
chúchòjèe

depend: it depends 看情况再说
kàn chíngkwàrng dzì shwōr

dessert 甜食
tyénshír

diabetic 糖尿病
tárng·nyàobìng

dialect 方言
fārngyén

dialling code 长途区号
chárngtú chēwhào

diamond 钻石
dzwànshír

diarrhoea 拉肚子
lādùdzir

diary 日记
rìrjèe

dictionary 字典
dzìrdyěn

die 死
sǐr

different 不同
bùtóng

difficult 困难
kùnnan

dining room 餐厅
tsāntīng

dinner wǎnfàn	晚饭	**down: down there** syàmyèn nàrr	下面那儿
direct jírjyēh	直接	**downstairs** lósyà	楼下
direction fārngsyàrng	方向	**dragon** lóng	龙
dirty dzārng	脏	**dream** mèrng	梦
disabled tsánfày	残废	**dress** (*woman's*) lyénēechéwn	连衣裙
disaster dzīnàn	灾难	**drink** (*noun*) yǐnlyào	饮料
disease jéebìng	疾病	**drink** (*verb*) hēr	喝
disgusting ěrsyīn	恶心	**drinking water** yǐnyòngshwǎy	饮用水
disinfectant syāodújèe	消毒剂	**drive** kīchēr	开车
distance jèwlée	距离	**driver** sīrjēe	司机
district (*in town*) chēw	区	**driving licence** jyàshǐrjírjào	驾驶执照
disturb dájyǎo	打搅	**drugstore** (*US*) yàofárng	药房
divorced léehūn	离婚	**drunk** hērdzwàyler	喝醉了
do dzwòr	做	**dry** gān	干
that'll do nicely jèr jyò syíngler	这就行了	**dry-cleaner** gānsyěedyèn	干洗店
doctor ēesherng	医生	**duck** yādzir	鸭子
dog gǒ	狗	**dynasty** cháo	朝
doll yárngwáwa	洋娃娃	**the Ming/Ch'ing Dynasty** Míngcháo/ Chīngcháo	明朝 / 清朝
dollar mǎy·yewén	美元		
door mén	门		

E

ear	ěrdwor	耳朵
early	dzǎo	早
earrings	ěrhwán	耳环
earth	túrǎrng	土壤
east	dōng	东
easy	róng·èe	容易
eat	chīr	吃
egg	jēedàn	鸡蛋
either . . . or . . .	bú shìr . . . jyòshir . . .	不是……就是……
elastic	sōngjǐndì	松紧带
elbow	gērborjǒ	胳膊肘
electric	dyèn	电
electricity	dyèn	电
elevator	dyèntēe	电梯
else: something else	byéder dōngsyee	别的东西
embassy	dàshírgwǎn	大使馆
emergency	jéeshìr	急事
emperor	hwárngdèe	皇帝
empty	kōng	空
end (*noun*)	jìntó	尽头
engaged (*toilet*)	yǒrén	有人
(*to be married*)	dìnghūnler	订婚了
engine	mǎdá	马达
England	Yīng·gérlán	英格兰
English (*language*)	Yīng·yěw	英语
English girl/woman	Yīng·gwór gū·nyárng/ fùněw	英国姑娘/妇女
Englishman	Yīng·gwor·ren	英国人
enough	gòler	够了
that's enough	gòler	够了
entrance	rùkǒ	入口
envelope	syìnfērng	信封
epileptic	dyēnsyén·bìngrén	癫痫病人
Europe	Ōjō	欧洲

evening 晚上
wǎnshàrng

every 每一个
mǎyéegèr

everyone 每一个人
mǎyéegèr rén

everything 所有东西
swóryǒ
dōngsyēe

everywhere 每个地方
mǎyger
dèefārng

excellent 好极了
hǎojéeler

exchange (*verb: money*) 兑换
dwàyhwàn

exchange rate 汇兑率
hwàydwàylèw

exciting 真来劲
jēn lííjìn

excuse me (*to get attention*) 劳驾
láo jyà
(*pardon?*) 请再说一遍好吗？
chǐng dzì
shwōr éebyèn,
hǎo ma?

exhibition 展览
jánlǎn

exit 出口
chūkǒ

expensive 贵
gwày

explain 解释
jyěshìr

eye 眼睛
yěnjīng

eye shadow 眼影
yényǐng

F

face 脸
lyěn

factory 工厂
gōngchǎrng

family 家庭
jyātíng

famous 有名
yǒmíng

fan (*cooling*) 风扇
fērngshàn

fantastic 很棒
hěn bàrng

far (away) 远
yewěn

farm 农场
nóngchǎrng

fashionable 时髦
shírmáo

fast 快
kwì

fat (*person*) 胖
pàrng

father 爸爸
bàba

faucet (*US*) 水龙头
shwǎylóngtó

faulty 有毛病
yǒ máobìng

favourite 最喜欢的
dzwày
syěehwān
der

February 二月
èr·yewèh

feel: I feel well 我感觉很好
wór gǎn·jewéh
hén hǎo
I feel unwell 我感觉不舒服
wór gǎn·jewéh
bù shūfu

felt-tip pen 软头笔
rwǎntóběe

fence 栅栏
jàlán

ferry 渡船
dùchwán

fever 发烧
fāshāo

few: few tourists 很少的游客
hén shǎoder
yókèr
a few 一些
ēesyēh

field 田地
tyéndèe

filling (*tooth*) 补牙
bǔyá

film (*for camera*) 胶卷
jyāojwěn
(*at cinema*) 电影
dyènyǐng

find 找到
jǎodào

finger 手指头
shǒ jírtou

finish (*verb*) 结束
jyéshù

fire 火
hwǒr

fire extinguisher 灭火器
myèh·hwǒrchèe

first 第一
dèe·ēe

first class 一等
ēeděrng

first name 名字
míngdzir

first aid 急救
jéejyò

fish 鱼
yéw

fit (*healthy*) 健康
jyènkārng

fizzy 有汽的
yǒchèeder

flash 闪光灯
shǎn·gwārng·
dērng

flat (*noun*) 单元
dān·yewén

flat (*adjective*) 平坦
píngtǎn

flavour 味道
wàydao

flea 跳蚤
tyàodzǎo

flight 航班
hárngbān

floor (*of room*) 地板
dèebǎn
(*storey*) 楼
ló

flower 花
hwā

flu 流感
lyógǎn

fly (*insect*) 苍蝇
tsārngying

fly (*verb*) 飞
fāy

folk music 民间音乐
mínjyēn
yīn·yewèh

follow 跟着
gēnjer

food 食物
shírwù

food poisoning 食物中毒
shírwù jòngdú

foot 脚
jyǎo

on foot 步行
bùsyíng

football 足球
dzúchyó

for: for you/me 为你/我
wày něe/wǒr

I'm all for it 我赞成
wǒr
dzànchérng

forbidden 禁止
jìnjǐr

Forbidden City 紫禁城
Dzǐrjìnchérng

foreigner 外国人
wìgwor·ren

foreign exchange certificate 外汇券
wìhwày·jwèn

forest 森林
sēnlín

forget 忘记
wàrngjèe

fork 叉子
chādzir

(*in road*) 岔路
chàlù

form (*to fill in*) 表
byǎo

fortnight 二星期
lyǎrng
syīngchee

forward (*mail*) 转交
jwǎnjyāo

fracture 裂缝
lyèfèrng

France 法国
Fǎgwór

free 自由
dzìryó

(*of charge*) 免费
myěnfày

French (*language*) 法语
Fáyěw

French fries 炸土豆条
já tǔdòtyáo

Friday 星期五
syīngcheewǔ

fridge 冰厢
bīngsyārng

fried noodles 炒面
chǎomyèn

fried rice 炒饭
chǎofàn

friend 朋友
pérngyǒ

friendship store 友谊商店
yǒ·ée
shārngdyèn

from: from Beijing to Shanghai 从北京到上海
tsóng Bǎyjīng
dào Shàrnghǐ

front (*part*) 前面
chyénmyèn

in front of 在……前面
dzì . . .
chyénmyèn

fruit 水果
shwáygwǒr

full
măn 满

fun: have fun!
hăo hāo wán! 好好玩！

funeral
dzàrnglĕe 葬礼

funny (*strange*)
chéegwì 奇怪
(*amusing*)
yŏ èesir 有意思

furniture
jyājèw 家具

further
gèrng yewĕn 更远

fuse
báosyĕnsīr 保险丝

G

garage
chèechēr syōlĕechù 汽车修理处
(*for parking*)
tíngchērchărng 停车场

garden
hwā·yewén 花园

garlic
dàswàn 大蒜

gas
máychèe 煤气
(*gasoline*)
chèeyó 汽油

gate
dàmén 大门

gay
găo tóngsyìnglyèn der 搞同性恋的

gear
chĭrlún 齿轮

gents (*toilet*)
nán tsèrswŏr 男厕所

genuine
jēnjèrngder 真正的

Germany
Dérgwór 德国

get (*obtain*)
dér dào 得到

can you tell me how to get to . . .?
nĕe nérng gàosu wŏr dzĕmmer dào . . . ma? 你能告诉我怎么到……吗？

get back (*return*)
hwáylí 回来

get off
syàchēr 下车

get up
chĕelí 起来

gin
jīnjyŏ 金酒

girl
nĕwhí 女孩

girlfriend
nĕwpérngyŏ 女朋友

give
găy 给

give back
hwán găy 还给

glad
gāosyìng 高兴

glass (*for drinking*)
bōrleebāy 玻璃杯
(*material*)
bōrlee 玻璃

glasses 眼镜
yěnjìng

gloves 手套
shǒtào

glue 胶水
jyāoshwǎy

go 去
chèw

go away 离开
léekī

go away! 滚！
gǔn!

Gobi Desert 戈壁滩
Gērbèetān

go in 进去
jìnchèw

go out 出去
chūchèw

go down 下去
syàchèw

go up 上去
shàrngchèw

go through 穿过
chwān·gwòr

God 上帝
Shàrngdèe

gold 黄金
hwárngjīn

good 好
hǎo

goodbye 再见
dzìjyèn

got: have you got . . .? 你有……吗？
née yǒ . . . ma?

government 政府
jèrngfǔ

grammar 语法
yéwfǎ

grandfather (*maternal*) 外公
wìgōng
(*paternal*) 爷爷
yéyeh

grandmother (*maternal*) 外婆
wìpór
(*paternal*) 奶奶
nīnī

grapefruit 柚子
yòdzir

grapes 葡萄
pútao

grass 草
tsǎo

grateful 感激
gǎnjēe

greasy 油腻
yónèe

green 绿色
lèwsèr

grey 灰色
hwāysèr

grocer 杂货店
dzáhwòrdyèn

ground floor 第一楼
dèe ēe ló

group 小组
syáodzǔ

guarantee 保修
bǎosyō

guest 客人
kèr·ren

guide 导游
dǎoyó

guidebook 导游手册
dǎoyó shǒtsèr

guitar
jéetā 吉他

gun (*pistol*)
shŏchyārng 手枪
(*rifle*)
chyārng 枪

H

hair
tófa 头发

haircut
lĕefà 理发

hairdresser
lĕefàdyèn 理发店

half
éebàn 一半
half an hour
bàn syăoshir 半小时

ham
hwórtwăy 火腿

hamburger
hànbăobāo 汉堡包

hammer
chwáydzir 锤子

hand
shŏ 手

handbag
shŏtéebāo 手提包

handkerchief
shŏjwèn 手绢

handle (*of door etc*)
báshŏ 把手

hand luggage
shŏtée syínglĕe 手提行李

handsome
yīngjèwn 英俊

happy
kwìlèr 快乐

harbour
gárngkŏ 港口

hard (*material*)
yìng 硬
(*difficult*)
nán 难

hat
màodzir 帽子

hate
hèn 恨

have
yŏ 有
I have to . . .
wór dăy . . . 我得……

hay fever
hwāfĕnrèr 花粉热

he
tā; (*see grammar*) 他

head
tó 头

headache
tótérng 头疼

headlights
chērtódērng 车头灯

health: your health!
jù nĕe jyènkārng 祝你健康

hear
tīngjyèn 听见

hearing aid
jùtīngchèe 助听器

heart
syīndzàrng 心脏

heart attack
syīnjēe gĕrngsèr 心肌梗塞

heat
rèr 热
heating
nwănchèe 暖气
heavy
jòng 重
heel (*of shoe*)
gērr 跟
(*of foot*)
jyăogēn 脚跟
helicopter
jírshērng fāyjēe 直升飞机
hello
née hăo 你好
help
bārngjù 帮助
help!
jyòmìng! 救命！
her (*possessive*)
tāder 她的
(*object*)
tā; (*see grammar*) 她
herbs (*cooking*)
dzwŏrlyào 佐料
(*medicine*)
tsăoyào 草药
here
jèrr 这儿
hers
tāder; (*see grammar*) 她的
hiccups
dăgér 打嗝
high
gāo 高
hill
shān 山
him
tā; (*see grammar*) 他
hip
túnbù 臀部
hire: for hire
chūdzū 出租
his
tāder; (*see grammar*) 他的
hit (*verb*)
dă 打
hitchhike
dābyènchēr 搭便车
hole
dòng 洞
holiday
jyàchēe 假期
(*public*)
jyéh·rìr 节日
home
jyā 家
at home
dzì jyā 在家
(*in my country*)
dzì wŏrmen gwórjyā 在我们国家
go home
hwáy jyā 回家
honey
fērngmèe 蜂蜜
Hong Kong
Syārnggărng 香港
hope (*verb*)
syēewàrng 希望
horrible
kĕr pà 可怕
horse
mă 马

hospital
ēe·yewèn 医院

hospitality
rèrchíng hàokèr 热情好客

hot
hěn rèr 很热
(*to taste*)
là 辣

hotel (*superior, for foreigners*)
fàndyèn 饭店
(*small*)
léwgwǎn 旅馆

hour
syǎoshír 小时

house
fárngdzir 房子

how?
dzěmmer 怎么

how are you?
née hǎo ma? 你好吗？

how are things?
éechyèh dō hǎo ma? 一切都好吗？

how many?
dwōrshao? 多少？

how much?
dwōrshao? 多少？

hungry: I'm hungry
wǒr èrler 我饿了

hurry up!
kwì dyǎrr! 快点！

hurt: it hurts
térng 疼

husband
jàrngfu 丈夫

I

I
wǒr; (*see grammar*) 我

ice
bīng 冰

ice cream
bīngchéelín 冰淇淋

idiot
shǎgwā 傻瓜

if
rúgwǒr 如果

ignition
dyénhwǒr 点火

ill
shērngbìngler 生病了

immediately
mǎshàrng 马上

important
jòngyào 重要

impossible
bù kěrnérng 不可能

in
dzì 在

in London
dzì Lúndūn 在伦敦

in English
yòng Yīngyěw 用英语

is he in?
tā dzì ma? 他在吗？

included
bāokwòr dzìnày 包括在内

India
Yìndù 印度

indigestion 消化不良
syāohwà bù lyárng

industry 工业
gōngyèh

infection 感染
gánrǎn

information 信息
syìnsyēe

injection 注射
jùshèr

injured 受伤了
shòshārngler

inner tube 内胎
nàytī

innocent 无辜
wúgū

insect 昆虫
kūnchóng

insect repellent 驱虫剂
chēwchóngjèe

insurance 保险
báosyěn

intelligent 聪明
tsōngming

interesting 有意思
yǒ èesir

invitation 邀请
yāochǐng

Ireland 爱尔兰
ìěrlán

iron (*metal*) 铁
tyěh
(*for clothes*) 熨斗
yèwndǒ

ironmonger 五金商店
wǔjīn shārngdyèn

island 岛
dǎo

it 它
tā

it is . . . 它是……
tā shìr . . .; (*see grammar*)

J

jack (*car*) 千斤顶
chyēnjīndǐng

jacket 上衣
shàrng·ēe

jade 玉
yèw

jam 果酱
gwǒrjyàrng

January 一月
ēe·yewèh

Japan 日本
Rìrben

jasmine tea 茉莉花茶
mòrlèehwā chá

jaw 下颚
syà èr

jazz 爵士音乐
jwéshìr yīn·yewèh

jeans 牛仔裤
nyódzǐkù

jewellery 首饰
shǒshìr

job 工作
gōngdzwòr

joke 笑话
syàohwà

journey 旅行
lěwsyíng

have a good journey! 一路顺风！
éelù shùnfērng!

jug 罐子
gwàndzir

juice 果汁
gwǒrjīr

July 七月
chēe·yewèh

junction (*road*) 交叉口
jyāochākǒ

June 六月
lyò·yewèh

just: just two 只要二个
jǐryào lyǎrnggèr

K

key 钥匙
yàoshir

kidney 肾
shèn
(*to eat*) 腰子
yāodzir

kill 杀
shā

kilo 公斤
gōngjīn

kilometre 公里
gōnglěe

kind 很好
hén hǎo

kiss 吻
wěn

kitchen 厨房
chúfárng

knee 膝盖
syēegì

knife 刀子
dāodzir

know 知道
jīrdào
(*person*) 认识
rènshìr
I don't know 我不知道
wǒr bù jīrdào

Korea: North Korea 北朝鲜
Bǎy Cháosyěn
South Korea 南朝鲜
Nán Cháosyěn

L

ladder 梯子
tēedzir

ladies (*room*) 女厕所
něw tsèrswǒr

lady 女士
něwshìr

lake 湖
hú

lamb 羊肉
yárng·rò

lamp 灯
dērng

language 语言
yěwyén

Laos 老挝
Lǎowōr

large 大
dà

last 最后
dzwàyhò

last year chèw·nyén	去年
late wǎn	晚
laugh dà syào	大笑
laundry (*to wash*) yào syěe der ēefu	要洗的衣服
(*place*) syěe·ēedyèn	洗衣店
law fǎlèw	法律
lawn tsǎopíng	草坪
lawyer lèwshīr	律师
laxative syèyào	泻药
lazy lǎn	懒
leaflet shwōrmíngshū	说明书
leak lò	漏
learn syewéh	学
leather péegér	皮革
leave (*behind*) dyōsyà	丢下
(*go away*) léekī	离开
(*forget*) bǎ . . . wàrngler	把……忘了
left dzwǒr	左
on the left (of) dzì . . . dzwǒrbyēn	在左边
left·handed dzwórpyědzir	左撇子
left luggage syínglěe jèetsúnchù	行李寄存处
leg twǎy	腿
lemon níngmérng	柠檬
lemonade níngmérng chèeshwǎy	柠檬汽水
lemon tea níngmérngchá	柠檬茶
lens (*camera*) jìngtó	镜头
less shǎo ēesyēh	少一些
lesson kèr	课
letter (*in mail*) syìn	信
letterbox syìnsyārng	信箱
library túshūgwǎn	图书馆
licence jírjào	执照
lid gìdzir	盖子
lie down tǎrngsyà	躺下
life shērnghwór	生活
lift (*elevator*) dyèntēe	电梯

light (*in room etc*) dērng 灯
have you got a light? jyèh ger hwŏr, syíng ma? 借个火，行吗？
light (*adjective*) chīng 轻
light bulb dērngpào 灯泡
lighter dáhwŏrjēe 打火机
like: I like . . . wór syĕehwān . . . 我喜欢……
I would like . . . wór syărng . . . 我想……
like (*as*) syàrng 象
lip dzwăychún 嘴唇
lipstick kŏhóng 口红
listen (to) tīng 听
litre shērng 升
little syăo 小
a little bit (of) ēe dyén dyen 一点点
live jù 住
liver gān 肝
living room kèrtīng 客厅
lock swŏr 锁
long chárng 长
a long time hén jyŏ 很久
look: look (at) kàn 看
look (*seem*) kànshàrngchèw 看上去
look like syàrng 象
look for jăo 找
look out! syăosyīn! 小心！
lorry kăchēr 卡车
lose dyōshīr 丢失
lost property office shīrwù jāolĭng chù 失物招领处
lot: a lot (of) syĕw dwōr 许多
loud dàshērng der 大声的
love ìchíng 爱情
love (*verb*) ì 爱
lovely (*person*) kĕr ì 可爱
(*thing*) hén hăo 很好
low dēe 低
luck yèwnchee 运气
good luck! jù hăo yèwn! 祝好运！

luggage 行李
syínglěe

lunch 午饭
wŭfàn

lungs 肺
fày

M

mad 疯了
fērngler

magazine 杂志
dzájìr

mail 信件
syìnjyèn

make 做
dzwòr

make·up 化妆品
hwàjwārngpĭn

man 男的
nánder

manager 经理
jīnglěe

Mandarin 普通话
pŭtōnghwà

many 很多
hěn dwōr

Mao Tse Tung jacket 中山装
jōngshānjwārng

map 地图
dèetú

March 三月
sān·yewèh

market 市场
shìrchărng

married 已婚的
ěehūnder

martial arts 武术
wŭshù

mascara 睫毛油
jyémáoyó

match (*light*) 火柴
hwǒrchí
(*sport*) 比赛
běe sì

material (*cloth*) 布
bù

matter: it doesn't matter 没关系
máy gwānsee

mattress 床垫
chwárng dyèn

May 五月
wŭ·yewèh

maybe 可能
kěrnérng

me 我
wǒr

me too 我也是
wór yěh shìr;
(*see grammar*)

meal 饭
fàn

measles 麻疹
májěn

meat 肉
rò

medicine 药
yào

meeting 会
hwày

melon 瓜
gwā

mend 修理
syōlěe

men's room (*US*) 男厕所
nán tsèrswǒr

menu
tsì pŭ 菜谱

message
kŏsyìn 口信

metal
jīnshŭ 金属

metre
mĕe 米

middle
jōngjyēn 中间

milk
nyónĭ 牛奶

mine
wŏrder; (*see grammar*) 我的

mineral water
kwàrng·chwénshwăy 矿泉水

minute
fēn 分

mirror
jìngdzir 镜子

Miss
syáojyĕh 小姐

miss (*train etc*)
wùchēr 误车

I miss you
wŏr hén syărng nyèn nĕe 我很想念你

mistake
tswòrwù 错误

modern
syèndì 现代

Monday
syīngchee·ēe 星期一

money
chyén 钱

Mongolia
Mérnggŭ 蒙古

Inner Mongolia
Nàymĕrng 内蒙

Outer Mongolia
Wìmĕrng 外蒙

month
yewèh 月

moon
yewèh·lyàrng 月亮

more
gèrng dwōr 更多

I've no more . . .
wŏr máy yŏ . . . ler 我没有……了

no more rice thanks
bú yào fàn ler 不要饭了

morning
dzăoshàrng 早上

mosquito
wéndzir 蚊子

mosquito net
wénjàrng 蚊帐

most (of)
dà dwōrshù 大多数

mother
māma 妈妈

motorbike
mórtwōrchēr 摩托车

motorway
gāosù gōnglù 高速公路

mountain
shān 山

mouse
láoshŭ 老鼠

moustache
syăohúdzir 小胡子

mouth
dzwăyba 嘴巴

movie
dyènyǐng — 电影

movie theater (*US*)
dyènyǐng yewèn — 电影院

Mr . . .
. . . syēnsherng — ……先生

Mrs . . .
. . . fūren — ……夫人

Ms . . .
. . . nĕwshìr — ……女士

much
dwōr — 多

muscle
jēerò — 肌肉

museum
bórwùgwăn — 博物馆

mushrooms
ɱórgu — 蘑菇

music
yīn·yewèh — 音乐

must: I/she must
wŏr/tā yīnggī — 我/她应该

my
wŏrder; (*see grammar*) — 我的

N

nail (*in wall*)
dīngdzir — 钉子

nail clippers
jĭrjyā dāo — 指甲刀

nail polish
jĭrjyā yó — 指甲油

nail polish remover
chèwdyào jĭrjyāyó der — 去掉指甲油的

naked
lwórtĕe — 裸体

name
míngdzìr — 名字

what's your name?
nĕe jyào shemmer míngdzìr? — 你叫什么名字？

my name is Jim
wŏr jyào Jim — 我叫 Jim

napkin
tsānjīn — 餐巾

nappy
nyàobù — 尿布

narrow
jĭ — 窄

nationality
gwórjée — 国籍

natural
dzìr·rán — 自然

near
lée . . . hĕnjìn — 离……很近

near here
dzì fùjìn — 在附近

the nearest . . .
dzwàyjìnder . . . — 最近的……

nearly
chàbudwōr — 差不多

necessary
bèeyào — 必要

neck
bórdzir — 脖子

necklace
syàrnglyèn — 项链

need: I need . . .
wŏr syēwyào . . . — 我需要……

needle
jēn 针

negative (*film*)
děepyèn 底片

Nepal
Néebór·ěr 尼泊尔

nervous
jǐnjárng 紧张

never
tsónglí bù 从来不

new
syīn 新

news
syīnwén 新闻

newspaper
bàojǐr 报纸

New Year
syīnnyén 新年

happy New Year!
Syīnnyénhǎo 新年好

New Zealand
Syīn Syēelán 新西兰

next
syà éegèr 下一个

next to . . .
dzì . . .
párngbyēn 在……旁边

nice
hén hǎo 很好

night
yèh 夜

nightdress
shwàyēe 睡衣

no
bù 不

I've no . . .
wǒr máy yǒ
. . . 我没有……

no rice thanks
bú yào fàn 不要饭

nobody
máyyǒ·rén 没有人

noise
dzàoyīn 噪音

noisy
hén chǎo 很吵

non·smoking
fāy syēeyēn
chēw 非吸烟区

normal
jèrngchárng 正常

north
bǎy 北

nose
béedzir 鼻子

not
bù; (*see grammar*) 不

notebook
běejèeběn 笔记本

nothing
máy yǒ
shemmer 没有什么

November
shír·ēe·yewèh 十一月

now
syèndzì 现在

number
hàomǎ 号码

nurse
hùshir 护士

O

October
shír·yewèh 十月

of
. . . der; (*see grammar*) ……的

office
bàn·gōngshìr 办公室

often
jīngchárng 经常

oil
yó 油

OK
hǎo 好

I'm OK
wǒr hí syíng 我还行

old (*person*)
lǎo 老

(*things*)
jyò 旧

how old are you?
něe dwōrdàler? 你多大了？

I'm 25 years old
wǒr èrshírwǔ swàyler 我二十五岁了

omelette
chǎojēedàn 炒鸡蛋

on
dzì . . . shàrngmyen 在……上面

one
ēe 一

onion
yárngtsōng 洋葱

only
jír yǒ 只有

open (*adjective*)
kīler 开了

open (*verb*)
kī 开

opera
gērjèw 歌剧

Peking opera
jīngjèw 京剧

operation
shǒshù 手术

opposite:
opposite the . . .
dzì . . . dwàymyèn 在……对面

optician
yěnjìngdyèn 眼镜店

or
hwòrjer 或者

orange (*fruit*)
gwǎrng gān 广柑

(*colour*)
jéwhwárngsèr 桔黄色

orchestra
gwǎnsyén yewèh·dwày 管弦乐队

other
byéder 别的

our(s)
wǒrmender; (*see grammar*) 我们的

out: she's out
tā bú dzì 她不在

outside
wìmyen 外面

over (*above*)
dzì . . . shàrngmyèn 在……上面

over (*finished*)
wánler 完了

over there
dzì nàrr 在那儿

P

package
bāogwǒr 包裹

packet (*of cigarettes etc*)
bāo 一包

paddy field
dàotyén 稻田

page
yèh 页

pagoda
tă 塔

pain
térng 疼

painful
térng 疼

painkiller
chèwtòngpyèn 去痛片

painting
hwà 画

panda
syóngmāo 熊猫

pants (*trousers*)
chárng kù 长裤

panties
sānjyăokù 三角裤

paper
jĭr 纸

parcel
bāogwŏr 包裹

pardon?
nĕe shwōrder shemmer? 你说的什么?

parents
fùmŭ 父母

park (*noun*)
gōng·yewén 公园

park (*car*)
tíng chēr 停车

parking lot (*US*)
tíngchērchărng 停车场

part
bùfen 部分

party (*celebration*)
wănhwày 晚会

party (*group*)
twántĕe 团体

pass (*mountain*)
gwānkŏ 关口

passport
hùjào 护照

path
syăolù 小路

pavement
rénsyíngdào 人行道

pavilion
tíngdzir 亭子

pay
fùchyén 付钱

peach
táodzir 桃子

peanuts
hwāshērng 花生

pear
lée 梨

peas
wāndò 豌豆

pedal
tàbăn 踏板

pedestrian crossing
rénsyíng hérngdào 人行横道

pen
gārngbĕe 钢笔

pencil
chyēnbĕe 铅笔

penicillin
chīngmáysù 青霉素

penknife
chyēnbĕedāo 铅笔刀

people
rén 人

pepper (*spice*)
hújyāo 胡椒
(*red/green*)
shìrdzirjyāo 柿子椒

per cent
bǐfēn jīr . . . 百分之……

perfect
hǎojéeler 好极了

perfume
syārngshwǎy 香水

period (*woman's*)
yewèh·jīng 月经

person
rén 人

petrol
chèeyó 汽油

petrol station
jyāyójàn 加油站

phone (*verb*)
dǎ dyènhwà 打电话

phone box
dyènhwàtíng 电话亭

phone number
dyènhwàhàomǎ 电话号码

photograph
jàopyèn 照片

photograph (*verb*)
jàosyàrng 照相

phrase book
dwàyhwà shǒtsèr 对话手册

pickpocket
páshǒ 扒手

piece
kwì; (*see grammar*) 块

pill
yàowán 药丸

pillow
jěntó 枕头

pin
byéjēn 别针

pineapple
bōrlwór 菠萝

pink
fěnhóng 粉红

pipe
gwǎndzir 管子
(*to smoke*)
yēndǒ 烟斗

pity: it's a pity
jēn kěrsyēe 真可惜

plane
fāyjēe 飞机

plant
jírwù 植物

plastic
sùlyào 塑料

plastic bag
sùlyàodì 塑料袋

plate
pándzir 盘子

platform (*station*)
jàntí 站台

play (*theatre*)
hwàjèw 话剧

play (*verb*)
wán 玩

pleasant
yéwkwì 愉快

please
chǐng 请

pleased
gāosyìng 高兴

pliers
chyéndzir 钳子

plug (*electric*) 插头
chātó
(*in sink*) 塞子
sīdzir
plum 李子
lěedzir
pocket 口袋
kǒdì
poison 毒
dú
police 警察
jǐngchá
policeman 警察
jǐngchá
police station 警察局
jǐngchájéw
polite 有礼貌
yó lěemào
politics 政治
jèrngjìr
polluted 污染了的
wūrǎnler der
poor 穷
chyóng
pop music 流行音乐
lyósyíng
yīn·yewèh
pork 猪肉
jūrò
possible 可能
kěrnérng
post (*verb*) 寄
jèe
postcard 明信片
míngsyìnpyèn
poster 招贴画
jāotyēhwà
post office 邮局
yójéw
potato 土豆
tǔdò
pound (*money*) 英镑
yīngbàrng
prawn 对虾
dwàysyā
pregnant 怀孕
hwíyèwn
prescription 处方
chǔfārng
present (*gift*) 礼物
lěewù
pretty 漂亮
pyàolyarng
price 价格
jyàgér
priest 神父
shénfù
prison 监狱
jyēnyèw
private 私人
sīren
problem 困难
kùnnan
pronounce 发音
fāyīn
pull 拉
lā
pump 泵
bèrng
puncture 刺破
tsìrpò
purple 紫色
dzǐrsèr
purse 钱包
chyénbāo
push 推
twāy

put
fàrng 放

pyjamas
shwày·ēe 睡衣

Q

question
wèntee 问题

queue
dwàywŭ 队伍

quick(ly)
kwì 快

quiet
ānjìng 安静

quite (*fairly*)
bĕejyào 比较

R

rabbit
tùdzir 兔子

radio
shōyīnjēe 收音机

railway
tyĕlù 铁路

rain
yĕw 雨

it's raining
syàyĕw ler 下雨了

raincoat
yĕw·ēe 雨衣

rape
chyárngjyēn 强奸

raspberry
mùmáy 木莓

rat
láoshŭ 老鼠

raw
shērng 生

razor
gwā húdāo 刮胡刀

razor blade
gwāhú dāopyèn 刮胡刀片

read
dú 读

ready
jŭnbày hăo 准备好

rear lights
hò chērdērng 后车灯

receipt
shōjèw 收据

reception (*hotel*)
jyēdìchù 接待处

record (*music*)
chàrngpyèn 唱片

record player
dyènchàrngjēe 电唱机

red
hóngsèr 红色

red·headed
hóng tófa der 红头发的

religion
dzōngjyào 宗教

remember: I remember
wŏr jèeder 我记得

rent (*verb*)
dzū 租

repair
syōlĕe 修理

repeat
chóngfù 重复

reservation 预订
yèwdìng

rest (*remaining*) 剩下的
shèrngsyà der

rest (*sleep*) 休息
syōsyee

restaurant 饭店
fàndyèn

restroom (*US*) 厕所
tsèrswǒr

reverse (*gear*) 倒车档
dàochēr
dǎrng

reverse charge call 对方付款
dwàyfārng
fùkwǎn

rheumatism 风湿病
fērngshīrbìng

rib 肋骨
làygǔ

rice (*cooked*) 饭
fàn
(*uncooked*) 米
měe

rice bowl 饭碗
fànwǎn

rice field 稻田
dàotyén

rich 有钱
yǒchyén

right (*side*) 右
yò
on the right (of) 在右边
dzì yòbyēn

right (*correct*) 对
dwày

ring (*on finger*) 戒指
jyèjir

river 河
hér

road 路
lù

roll (*bread*) 面包卷
myènbāo
jewěn

roof 房顶
fárngdǐng

room 房间
fárng·jyēn

rope 绳子
shérngdzir

rose 玫瑰
máygwày

route 路线
lùsyèn

rubber 橡胶
syàrngjyāo
(*eraser*) 橡皮
syàrngpée

rubber band 橡皮筋
syàrngpéejīn

rubbish (*refuse*) 垃圾
lājēe

rucksack 背包
bàybāo

rude 粗鲁
tsūlǔ

rug 小地毯
syǎo dèetǎn

ruins 废墟
fàysyēw

rum 兰姆酒
lánmújyǒ

run 跑
pǎo

Russia 俄国
Érgwór

S

sad 难过
nán·gwòr

safe 安全
ānchwén

safety pin 别针
byéjēn

salad 色拉
sèrlā

salt 盐
yén

same 一样
éeyàrng

sandals 凉鞋
lyárngsyéh

sandwich 三明治
sānmíngjìr

sanitary towel 卫生巾
wàyshērngjīn

Saturday 星期六
syīngcheelyò

sauce 汁
jīr

sausage 香肠
syārngchárng

say 说
shwōr

scarf (*neck*) 围巾
wáyjīn

school 学校
syewéh·syào

scissors 剪刀
jyĕndāo

Scotland 苏格兰
Sūgérlán

screwdriver 螺丝刀
lwórsīrdāo

scroll 画轴
hwàjó

sea 海
hǐ

seaside: at the seaside 在海边
dzì hǐbyēn

seat 座位
dzwòrway

seatbelt 安全带
ānchwéndì

second (*in time*) 秒
myăo

see 看见
kànjyen

sell 卖
mì

sellotape (*R*) 透明胶带
tòmíng jyāodì

send 送
sòng
(*letter*) 寄
jèe

separate 分开
fēnkı

September 九月
jyŏ·yewèh

serviette 餐巾
tsānjīn

several 几个
jĕeger

sew 缝
férng

sexy 性感
syìnggăn

shade: in the shade dzı yīnlyárng chù 在荫凉处
shampoo syěefàjīng 洗发精
share (*verb*) fēnsyǎrng 分享
shaving brush syōmyènshwā 修面刷
shaving foam gwā hú pàomòr 刮胡泡沫
she tā; (*see grammar*) 她
sheet chwárngdān 床单
ship chwán 船
shirt chènshān 衬衫
shoe laces syédì 鞋带
shoe polish syéyó 鞋油
shoe repairer syōsyédyèn 修鞋店
shoes syéh 鞋
shop shārngdyèn 商店
go shopping chèw mǐ dōngsēe 去买东西
short (*person*) ǐ 矮
(*time*) dwǎn 短
shorts dwǎnkù 短裤
shoulder jyēnbǎrng 肩膀
shower (*wash*) línyèw 淋浴
shy hìsyō 害羞
Siberia Syēebórlèeyà 西伯利亚
sidewalk rénsyíngdào 人行道
signature chyēnmíng 签名
silk sīrchó 丝绸
Silk Road sīrchó jīr lù 丝绸之路
silver yín 银
silver foil yín bór 银箔
similar syārngsìr 相似
simple (*easy*) jyěndān 简单
since (*time*) dzìr tsóng . . . 自从……
sing chàrnggēr 唱歌
Singapore Syīnjyāpōr 新加坡
single (*unmarried*) wàyhūn 未婚
sister jyěmày 姐妹
sit down dzwòrsyà 坐下

size
chǐrtsùn 尺寸

skin
péefū 皮肤

skinny
tì shò 太瘦

skirt
chéwndzir 裙子

sky
tyēn kōng 天空

sleep
shwàyjyào 睡觉

sleeper
wòrpù 卧铺

sleeping bag
shwàydì 睡袋

sleeping pill
ānmyényào 安眠药

sleepy: I'm sleepy
wǒr kùnler 我困了

slide (*phot*)
hwàndērngpyèn 幻灯片

slim
myáotyao 苗条

slippers
twōrsyéh 拖鞋

slow(ly)
màn 慢

small
syǎo 小

smell (*verb*)
wén 闻

smile
syào 笑

smoke (*noun*)
yēn 烟

smoke (*verb*)
syēeyēn 吸烟

snake
shér 蛇

snow
syewěh 雪

so (*big, slow etc*)
jèrmer 这么

soap
fáydzào 肥皂

socket
chādzwòr 插座

socks
wàdzir 袜子

soft
rwǎn 软

soft drink
rwán yǐnlyào 软饮料

sole (*of shoe*)
syéděe 鞋底

some
eesyēh 一些

somebody
yǒrén 有人

something
yǒsyēh dōngsyēe 有些东西

sometimes
yǒ shír 有时

son
érdzir 儿子

song
gēr 歌

soon
bù jyǒ 不久

sore: I've got a sore throat
wǒr hólong térng 我喉咙疼

sorry
dwàybuchěe 对不起

I'm sorry
dwàybuchěe 对不起

so-so
mămahūhu 马马虎虎

soup
tārng 汤

sour
swān 酸

south
nán 南

soy sauce
jyàrng·yó 酱油

spanner
hwór bānshŏ 活扳手

spare parts
língjyèn 零件

spark plug
hwŏrhwā sī 火花塞

speak
jyărng 讲

do you speak ...?
née jyărng ... ma? 你讲……吗？

speed limit
sùdù syènjìr 速度限制

spider
jīrjū 蜘蛛

spoke
fútyáo 辐条

spoon
syăosháorr 小勺

sport
yèwndòng 运动

spring (*season*)
chūntyēn 春天

square (*in town*)
gwárngchărng 广场

stairs
lótēe 楼梯

stamp
yópyào 邮票

star
syīngsying 星星

station
hwŏrchērjàn 火车站

stay (*in hotel etc*)
jù 住

steak
nyópí 牛排

steal
tō 偷

steamed roll
hwājwărr 花卷

steep
hén dŏ 很陡

steering wheel
fārngsyàrng·pán 方向盘

still (*adverb*)
rérngrán 仍然

stockings
chárngtŏngwà 长统袜

stomach
wày 胃

stomach ache
wàytérng 胃疼

stone
shírto 石头

stop
chērjàn 车站

stop (*verb*)
tíngjĭr 停止

stop!
tíngsyà! 停下！

store
shārngdyèn 商店

storm
bàofērng·yĕw 暴风雨

story
gùshir 故事

straight ahead
èejír cháochyén 一直朝前

strange (*odd*)
chéegwì 奇怪

strawberry
tsǎomáy 草莓

stream
syǎosyēe 小溪

street
jyēh 街

string
syèeshérng 细绳

stroke (*attack*)
jòng fērng 中风

strong
jwàrng 壮
(*drink*)
lyèh 烈
(*material*)
jyēshir 结实

student
syewéh·shērng 学生

stupid
bèn 笨

suburbs
jyāochēw 郊区

suddenly
tūrán 突然

sugar
tárng 糖

suit
syēejwārng 西装

suitcase
shǒtéesyārng 手提箱

summer
syàtyēn 夏天

sun
tìyárng 太阳

sunburn
shì hāy 晒黑

Sunday
syīngcheetyēn 星期天

sunglasses
tìyárngjìng 太阳镜

sunstroke
jòngshǔ 中暑

suntan lotion
fárngshìjèe 防晒剂

supermarket
chāojée shìrchǎrng 超级市场

surname
syìng 姓

sweater
máo·ēe 毛衣

sweet
tárng 糖
(*to taste*)
tyén 甜

swim
yóyǒng 游泳

swimming costume
yóyǒng·ēe 游泳衣

swimming pool
yóyǒngchír 游泳池

swimming trunks
yóyǒngkù 游泳裤

switch (*electric*)
kīgwān 开关

T

table
jwōrdzir 桌子

table tennis
pīngpārngchyó 乒乓球

Taiwan
Tíwān 台湾

take
ná 拿

take away (*remove*)
nádzǒ 拿走

talk
shwōrhwà 说话

tall
gāo 高

Taoism
Dàojyā 道家

tap
shwǎylóngtó 水龙头

tape (*cassette*)
tsírdì 磁带

taste
wàyr 味

taxi
chūdzūchēr 出租车

tea
chá 茶

teach
jyào 教

teacher
lǎoshīr 老师

team
dwày 队

teapot
cháhú 茶壶

telegram
dyènbào 电报

telephone
dyènhwà 电话

television
dyènshìr 电视

temple
myào 庙

tennis
wǎrngchyó 网球

tent
jàrngpérng 帐篷

Terra Cotta Army
Bīngmáyǒng 兵马俑

terrible
jēn dzāogāo 真糟糕

terrific
bàrngjéeler 棒极了

Thailand
Tìgwór 泰国

than
běe . . . gèrng 比……更

uglier than . . .
běe . . . gèrng nánkàn 比……更难看

thank
syèh·syeh 谢谢

thank you
syèh·syeh 谢谢

that
nàger 那个

that one
nàger 那个

the
jèr, nà; (*see grammar*) 这，那

theatre
jèw·yewèn 剧院

their(s)
tāmender; (*see grammar*) 他们的

them
tāmen; (*see grammar*) 他们

then
nà shír 那时
(*after that*)
ránhò 然后
there
nàrr 那儿
there is/are
yǒ . . . 有……
is/are there . . .?
yǒ . . . ma? 有……吗？
there isn't/aren't . . .
máy yǒ . . . 没有……
thermometer
wēndùjèe 温度计
thermos flask
rèrshwǎypíng 热水瓶
these
jèrsyēh 这些
they
tāmen; (*see grammar*) 他们
thick
hò 厚
thief
syǎo tō 小偷
thigh
dàtwǎy 大腿
thin (*thing*)
báo 薄
(*person*)
shò 瘦
thing
dōngsyee 东西
think
syǎrng 想
thirsty: I'm thirsty
wǒr kókěr 我口渴
this (*adjective*)
jèr 这
this one
jèrger 这个
those
nàsyēh 那些
thread
syèn 线
throat
hólóng 喉咙
through
jīnggwòr 经过
throw
rērng 扔
throw away
rērngdyào 扔掉
thunderstorm
láyyěw 雷雨
Thursday
syīngcheesìr 星期四
Tibet
Syēedzàrng 西藏
ticket
pyào 票
tie (*necktie*)
lǐngdì 领带
tight
jǐn 紧
tights
lyénkùwà 连裤袜
time
shírjyēn 时间
on time
jǔnshír 准时
what time is it?
jéedyěn ler? 几点了？
timetable
shírjyēnbyǎo 时间表
tin opener
gwànto chěedzir 罐头起子

tip (*money*)
syǎofày 小费
tire (*US*)
lúntī 轮胎
tired
lày 累
tissues
kójīr 口纸
to
dào 到
I'm going to Beijing/the station
wǒr yào dào Bǎyjīng/chērjàn chèw 我要到北京/车站去
tobacco
yēnsīr 烟丝
today
jīntyēn 今天
toe
jyáojīr 脚趾
together
ēechēe 一起
toilet
tsèrswǒr 厕所
toilet paper
shójīr 手纸
tomato
syēehóngshìr 西红柿
tomorrow
míngtyēn 明天
tongue
shérto 舌头
tonight
jīntyen wǎnsharng 今天晚上
tonsillitis
byěntáosyèn·yén 扁桃腺炎
too (*also*)
yěh 也
too big
tì dà 太大
not too much
bú tì dwōr 不太多
too much
tì dwōr 太多
tooth
yá 牙
toothache
yáterng 牙疼
toothbrush
yáshwā 牙刷
toothpaste
yágāo 牙膏
torch
shōdyèntōng 手电筒
tourist
yókèr 游客
towel
máojīn 毛巾
town
chérngshìr 城市
track (*US: station*)
jàntí 站台
traditional
chwántōng 传统
traffic
jyāotōng 交通
traffic jam
jyāotōng dǔsī 交通堵塞
traffic lights
hónglèw dērng 红绿灯
train
hwǒrchēr 火车
translate
fānèe 翻译

travel agent 旅行社
lěwsyíngshèr

traveller's cheque 旅行支票
lěwsyíng jīrpyào

tree 树
shù

tremendous 好极了
hăojéeler

trip 旅游
lěwyó

trousers 长裤
chárng kù

true 真的
jēnder

trunk (*US: car*) 行李箱
syíngleesyārng

try 试试
shìr shir

T·shirt T恤衫
T syèw·shān

Tuesday 星期二
syīngchee·èr

tunnel 隧道
swàydào

tweezers 镊子
nyèdzir

tyre 轮胎
lúntī

U

ugly 难看
nánkàn

umbrella 雨伞
yéwsăn

uncle 叔叔
shūshu

under 在……下面
dzì . . . syàmyèn

underpants 裤衩
kùchă

understand 明白
míngbí

United States 美国
Măygwór

university 大学
dàsyewéh

unpleasant 不怎么样
bù dzĕmmer·yàrng

until 直到
jírdào

up: up there 在那儿
dzı nàr

upstairs 在楼上
dzı lóshàrng

urgent 紧急
jĭnjée

us 我们
wŏrmen; (*see grammar*)

use 用
yòng

useful 有用
yŏyòng

usually 通常
tōngchárng

V

vaccination 种牛痘
jòng·nyódò

valid
yǒsyào 有效

valley
shāngǔ 山谷

van
syǎo yèwnhwòrchēr 小运货车

vanilla
syārngtsǎo 香草

vase
hwāpíng 花瓶

VD
syìngbìng 性病

veal
syǎonyóròu 小牛肉

vegetables
shūtsì 蔬菜

vegetarian
chīrsù der 吃素的

very
fāycharng 非常

very much
fāychárng 非常

video
lùsyàrng·jēe 录相机

Vietnam
Yewèh·nán 越南

village
tsūndzir 村子

vinegar
tsù 醋

visa
chyēnjèrng 签证

visit (*place*)
tsān·gwān 参观
(*people*)
bìfǎrng 拜访

voice
shērng·yīn 声音

W

waist
yāo 腰

wait
děrng 等

waiter
jāodì 招待

waitress
jāodì 招待

wake up (*oneself*)
syǐngler 醒了

Wales
Wāyěrshìr 威尔士

walk (*verb*)
dzǒlù 走路

walkman (*R*)
syòjēn fàrngyīnjēe 袖珍放音机

wall
chyárng 墙

the Great Wall of China
Chárngchérng 长城

wallet
chyénbāo 钱包

want
yào 要

I want . . .
wǒr yào . . . 我要……

do you want . . .?
něe yào . . . ma? 你要……吗？

war
jànjērng 战争

warm
nwǎnhwór 暖和

wash
syĕe 洗

washbasin
syéelyĕnchír 洗脸池

washing powder
syĕe·ēefĕn 洗衣粉

wasp
hwárngfērng 黄蜂

watch (*for time*)
shóbyăo 手表

watch (*verb*)
kàn 看

water
shwăy 水

way: this way (*like this*)
jèr·yàrng 这样

can you tell me the way to the . . .?
nĕe nérng gàosù wŏr chèw . . . der lù ma? 你能告诉我去……的路吗？

we
wŏrmen; (*see grammar*) 我们

weak
rwòr 弱
(*tea*)
dàn 淡

weather
tyēnchèe 天气

wedding
hūnlĕe 婚礼

Wednesday
syīngcheesān 星期三

week
syīngchēe 星期

weekend
jōmòr 周末

weight
jònglyàrng 重量

welcome!
hwānyíng! 欢迎！

welcome: you're welcome
bú kèrchee 不客气

well: he's well/not well
tā shēnti hén hăo/bù hăo 他身体很好/不好

well (*adverb*)
hén hăo 很好

west
syēe 西

Western·style
syēeshìr 西式

wet
shīr 湿

what?
shémmer? 什么？

what's this?
jèr shìr shemmer? 这是什么？

what is . . .?
. . . shir shemmer? ……是什么？

wheel
lúndzir 轮子

when?
shémmer shírhò? 什么时候？

where?
nărr? 哪儿？

which
nă·éegèr 哪一个

white
bísèr 白色

who?
shäy? 谁？
whose: whose is this?
jèr shir sháyder? 这是谁的？
why?
wàyshemmer? 为什么？
wide
kwān 宽
wife
chēedzir 妻子
win
yíng 赢
wind
fērng 风
window
chwārnghu 窗户
windscreen
dǎrngfērng bōrlee 挡风玻璃
wine
pútaojyǒ 葡萄酒
winter
dōngtyēn 冬天
wire
tyěsīr 铁丝
with
hér . . . ēechěe 和……一起
without
máyyǒ 没有
without ice
bú yào bīng 不要冰
woman
fùněw 妇女
wonderful
tì hǎoler 太好了
wood
mùtou 木头
wool
yárngmáo 羊毛
word
tsír 词
work
gōngdzwòr 工作
work (*verb*)
gōngdzwòr 工作
it's not working
hwìler 坏了
world
shìrjyèh 世界
worse
gèrng dzāo 更糟
wrench
bānshǒ 扳手
wrist
shǒwàn 手腕
write
syěh 写
wrong
tswòr 错

Y

Yangtze Gorges
Chárngjyārng sānsyá 长江三峡
Yangtze River
Chárngjyārng 长江
year
nyén 年
yellow
hwárngsèr 黄色
Yellow River
Hwárnghér 黄河
Yellow Sea
Hwárnghǐ 黄海

yes
shìrder; (*see grammar*) 是的

yesterday
dzwórtyēn 昨天

yet: not yet
hí máyner 还没呢

yoghurt
swānnĭ 酸奶

you
nĕe 你
(*plural*)
nĕemen; (*see grammar*) 你们

young
nyénchīng 年轻

young people
nyénchīngrén 年轻人

your(s)
nĕeder 你的
(*plural*)
nĕemender; (*see grammar*) 你们的

Z

zero
líng 零

zip
lālyèn 拉链

zoo
dòngwù·yewén 动物园

GRAMMAR

STRUCTURE

In the south-east of China, Pidgin English was used for three hundred years by foreigners trading with the Chinese. In some ways, colloquial Chinese and Pidgin English are like each other, in their simple structure, small vocabulary, and wide use of a few basic verbs:

wǒr chèw kàn kàn
(I go look look)
I'll go and have a look

A Chinese sentence is like a string of beads or a row of pebbles, chosen and arranged for conciseness and clarity. Nothing declines or conjugates. Word order is similar to English, subject – verb – object:

wǒr yào jày ger
I want this one

There are no *ARTICLES*, no words for **a** and **the** in Chinese, so for example:

yínháng
the bank, a bank, the banks, banks

fùjìn yǒ yínháng ma?
(neighbourhood there is bank 'question word'?)
is there a bank near here?

SINGULAR and *PLURAL* forms are not distinguished, so for example:

rén
man, men

If need be, the words for **one** or **some, many** etc, are added:

ēe gèr rén
one man, a man

hěn dwōr rén
a lot of men

GRAMMAR

An *ADJECTIVE* is often introduced by the word 'hěn' **very**:

hén hǎo
(very good)
excellent

hén hǎo chīr
(very good eat)
delicious

hěn pyàolyàrng
(very pretty)
lovely

The verb *TO BE* is normally omitted in basic sentences like:

tā hén hǎo
(he very good)
he's an excellent person

tsì hén hǎo chīr
(food very good eat)
the food is delicious

fērngjíng hěn pyàolyàrng
(scenery very pretty)
the scenery is splendid

When the word order is changed, with the adjective coming before the noun, the word 'der' is added:

hén hǎo chīr der tsì
(very good eat 'der' vegetables)
delicious vegetables

hěn pyàolyàrng der fērngjǐng
(very pretty 'der' scenery)
splendid scenery

The word 'der' can be added to a verb in the following way:

dzǒder hěn màn
(go 'der' very slow)
we're going very slowly!

gwòrder hěn kwìlèr
(pass 'der' very happy)
we're having a very happy time

GRAMMAR

The *COMPARATIVE* is often understood from the context:

nă-ēeger hăo?	jèrger hăo
(which one good)	*(this one good)*
which is better?	**this is better**

Than is 'bĕe':

jèrger bĕe nàyger hăo
(this than that good)
this is better than that

For *SUPERLATIVES* the word 'dzwày' **most** is used:

syăo Wárng dzwày pàrng
(little Wang most fat)
little Wang is the fattest

PERSONAL PRONOUNS are:

wŏr	**I/me**	wŏrmen	**we/us**
nĕe	**you**	nĕemen	*(pl)* you
tā	**he/him, she/her**	tāmen	**they/them**

There is a respect form of **you**, 'nín', used in speaking to old or senior people:

nín chĭng zwòr
(you please sit)
please have a seat

Pronouns are often left out in Chinese:

jăo sháy?	jăo pérngyŏ
(seek who?)	*(seek friends)*
who are you looking for?	**I'm looking for my friends**

jīntyēn hăo rèr
(today good hot)
it's very hot today

Pronouns are used for emphasis:

wŏr bú hwày Hànyĕw kĕrshìr tā hwày
(I not can Chinese but he can)
I don't speak Chinese but he does

GRAMMAR

POSSESSIVE ADJECTIVES and *POSSESSIVE PRONOUNS* are formed by adding 'der' to the pronoun:

wŏrder	**my/mine**
nĕeder	**your/yours**
tāder	**his, her/hers, its**
wŏrmender	**our/ours**
nĕemender	**your/yours** (*pl*)
tāmender	**their/theirs**

tāder jyā
his home

nà shìr wŏrmender
that's ours

VERBS do not change at all – there is only one form. If need be, other words are added to make the sense clear. For example:

lí

can mean all of:

come, comes, came, will come, come!

tā lí
he/she comes, he/she came, he/she will come

tā dzwórtyēn lí
he/she came yesterday

Normally the context will make the time reference of a verb clear. Words like **tomorrow** or **yesterday** remove any ambiguity.

EXPRESSING THE PRESENT

tā hĕn lày
(he very tired)
he's very tired

nĕe zwòr shemmer?
(you do what)
what are you doing?

wŏr bù syĕehwān yīn-yewèh
(I not like music)
I don't like music

EXPRESSING THE FUTURE

míngtyēn dzŏ
(tomorrow go)
we're off tomorrow

wŏr bú chèw
(I not go)
I'm not going

GRAMMAR

EXPRESSING THE PAST (see also *PARTICLES*)

tā zwórtyēn lí
(he yesterday come)
he came yesterday

máy yǒ chèw
(not have go)
I didn't go

YES/NO

Although there are words that can be used for **yes/no**, the usual way to say **yes** or **no** is by repeating a word in the question:

něe hwày yóyǒng ma?
(you can swim 'question word'?)
can you swim?

hwày!
(can)
yes

For **no** you add 'bù':

něe lí ma?
(you come 'question word'?)
are you coming?

bù lí
(not come)
no

QUESTIONS are formed by adding 'ma':

něe yào chèw
(you want go)
you want to go

něe yào chèw ma?
(you want go 'question word'?)
do you want to go?

Another way of asking questions is the form:

lày bú lày?
(tired not tired?)
are you tired?

márng bù márng?
(busy not busy)
are you busy?

GRAMMAR

Special question words:

who?	sháy? sháy yào chèw? *(who want go?)*	**who wants to go?**
what?	shemmer? shwōr shemmer? *(say what?)*	**what are you saying?**
when?	shemmer shírhò? shemmer shírhò yŏ kòng? *(what time have free?)*	**when are you free?**
what time?	jée dyĕn? jée dyén dzŏ? *(what time go?)*	**what time are we going?**
where?	năırr? tā dzì nărr? *(he at where?)*	**where is he?**
	tā dào nărr? *(he to where?)*	**where has he gone to?**
why?	wày shemmer? wày shemmer bú chèw? *(why not go?)*	**why aren't you going?**
how long?	dwōrshăo shírjyēn? yào dwōrshăo shírjyēn? *(want how much time?)*	**how long does it take?**
how much?	dwōrshăo? jèr dwōrshăo chyén? *(this how much money?)*	**how much is this?**
how many?	jĕeger? née yó jĕeger syăohí? *(you have how many children?)*	**how many children do you have?**

To form ***NEGATIVES*** the main word for **not** is 'bù':

tā bù lí
(he not come)
he's not coming

But before 'yŏ' **have**, **not** is 'máy':

née yŏ máy yŏ chyén?	máy yŏ
(you have not have money?)	*(not have)*
do you have money?	**no, I don't (have any)**

When referring to the past **not** is 'máy':

tā máy lí
(he not come)
he didn't come

NUMBERS do not immediately precede nouns, as they do in English. A *COUNT WORD* must be inserted. This resembles the English **a slice of bread, a bar of chocolate, a packet of crisps**. Often, the count word is 'gèr':

sān gèr rén	ée gèr pínggwŏr
3 people	**1 apple**

But sometimes 'gèr' will not do. Long, thin objects may have the count word 'tyáo':

ēe tyáo hér	ēe tyáo shér
a river	**a snake**

Flat, thin objects may use 'jārng':

ēe jārng jĭr	lyărng jārng jwōrdzir
a piece of paper	**two tables**

Other useful count words are:

wày:	ée wày syēnshērng	sìr wày tìtì
	a gentleman	**four ladies**
kwì:	ēe kwì . . .	
	a portion/piece (of bread, soap etc)	
wăn:	ēe wăn	
	a bowl (of rice/soup etc)	

Two is only 'èr' when counting:

ēe èr sān sìr
one two three four

Otherwise, it is 'lyărng':

lyărng gèr pérngyŏ
2 friends

GRAMMAR

Chinese uses *PARTICLES* to modify the meaning of a verb.

'ler' **finish** is added for a process that has reached completion:

chēr lí ler
(bus come finish)
the bus is here

shwǎy kī ler
(water boil finish)
the water's boiling

dào ler
(arrive finish)
here we are!

'hǎo' **good, ready** is added for a job that is done:

jǔnbày hǎo
(prepare ready)
it's ready

bàn hǎo
(negotiate ready)
it's arranged

syōlée hǎo
(repair ready)
it's fixed

'ba' is added for a suggestion:

dzǒ ba!
let's be off!

'ner' means **what about?**:

wǒr chèw, něe ner?
I'm going, what about you?

'gwòr' **pass** is used for things one has done:

něe chèwgwòr Mǎygwór ma?
(you go 'pass' America 'question word'?)
have you been to America?

OF is translated using 'der' (which is equivalent to **'s**):

lǎo Wárng der jyā
Lao Wang's home

tāder jyā
his house

léwgwǎn der míngdzir
the name of the hotel

CONVERSION TABLES

metres
1 metre = 39.37 inches or 1.09 yards

kilometres
1 kilometre = 0.62 or approximately 5/8 mile

to convert kilometres to miles: divide by 8 and multiply by 5

kilometres:	2	3	4	5	10	100
miles:	1.25	1.9	2.5	3.1	6.25	62.5

miles
to convert miles to kilometres: divide by 5 and multiply by 8

miles:	1	3	5	10	20	100
kilometres:	1.6	4.8	8	16	32	160

kilos
1 kilo = 2.2 or approximately 11/5 pounds

to convert kilos to pounds: divide by 5 and multiply by 11

kilos:	4	5	10	20	30	40
pounds:	8.8	11	22	44	66	88

pounds
1 pound = 0.45 or approximately 5/11 kilo

litres
1 litre = approximately 1¾ pints or 0.22 gallons

Celsius
to convert to Fahrenheit: divide by 5, multiply by 9, add 32

Celsius:	10	15	20	25	28	30	34
Fahrenheit:	50	59	68	77	82	86	93

Fahrenheit
to convert Fahrenheit to Celsius: subtract 32, multiply by 5, divide by 9